MONA K. SMITH

WHY DO THEY LISTEN WHEN YOU SAY IT?

Miss Mona's
TIPS & TECHNIQUES FOR
MOTHERS, FATHERS, &
CAREGIVERS

Copyright © 2021 Mona K. Smith
All Rights Reserved

Year of the Book
135 Glen Avenue
Glen Rock, PA 17327

Print ISBN: 978-1-64649-101-8
Ebook ISBN: 978-1-64649-102-5

No part of this publication may be reproduced, distributed, or transmitted in any form or by any means, including photocopying, recording, or other electronic or mechanical methods, without the prior written permission of the publisher, except in the case of brief quotations embodied in critical reviews and certain other noncommercial uses permitted by copyright law.

The stories in this book are true, although the names have been changed to protect the innocent (and in some cases those who aren't so innocent). A few stories and characters are a conglomeration of more than one person or incident.

Dedication

To my husband, Mike, who encouraged me to write before I had ever thought to. You cheered me on, and pushed me over the hills when I was too afraid to share my words. Without you there would be no book.

To my kids, my people, who inspire me to do better and be better each and every day. Because of you four, I finished the book... if for no other reason than to be a good example to you that we finish what we start.

And to all the preschoolers I have taught, who in turn taught me and kept me on my toes, making me grow my own "Mary Poppins Bag" of tricks.

Contents

Introduction 1

1 | Lead with Love 5

2 | The Perfect Parent (Not) 11

3 | 1, 2, Cha-Cha-Cha – Routines, Consistency & Follow Through 15

4 | Bite Your Tongue – Communication Tips for Talking with Your Child 29

5 | Flushing the Diaper – Potty Training 47

6 | Preschool or Not – Sometimes It Is a Fact of Life 55

7 | No More Static Cling – Separation Anxiety Tips for an Easier Goodbye 61

8 | Tantrums, Swearing, and Fighting, Oh My! 71

9 | It's Not the Monster Under the Bed 87

10 | A Stranger in My House – My Teenager Doesn't Talk to Me Anymore 95

11 | It's All About You (Sometimes) 101

12 | Fun 107

13 | Last Thoughts 113

Miss Mona's
Method MasterClass

Does your child listen to you?

Are you feeling frantic and overwhelmed?

Master Miss Mona's methods and techniques
in this fast and fun MasterClass.

Her 30-year experience with parents and children
has formed methods that work wonders...
so you can have a peaceful, happy home!

---

www.MissMonasMethod.com

$100 discount for book owners

Introduction

> *"And suddenly you know…*
> *It's time to start something new and*
> *trust the magic of new beginnings."*
>
> —Meister Eckhart

Thank you for choosing my book. It tells me something about you – it tells me you love your children and want what's best for them.

This book is for parents and caregivers who are looking for common-sense, jargon-free advice. Parenting books are usually written by "experts" with a long string of letters after their names, but that word "experts" sends me running for the hills. In my experience, experts try to scare parents and make them feel like they're doing it all wrong.

I don't like to feel that way and I don't want to make you feel that way either. Plus, I'm going to bet you're not doing it wrong; you just need help to get through the rough patches. We all do.

As a preschool teacher, I get to see parent and child interactions every day, observing mostly wonderful family moments. But there are difficult times as well. Making small positive changes in *our behavior* can make huge differences in our children's behavior, causing more happiness for everyone.

When my own children would get upset at me for scolding them or putting them in time-out, often they would say, "You don't love me." I would tell them, "If I didn't love you, I would let you do whatever you wanted." When done in a firm but not harsh way, discipline is love.

In these pages you will discover tips to help you deal with sleepless nights, the perils of potty training, happy goodbyes, and maybe even taking *your* temper out of your child's temper tantrum.

Having to correct your children does not mean you're mean. It doesn't imply that you don't love your kid, or that your child is bad. It merely says you have normal children who need guidance.

The tips and techniques in the following chapters are tried and true. I have been using them for over 33 years with my own children as well as my preschool students. Try them out, and give them a good chance, because it can take time. Don't change up everything all at once. We have to build new habits a little at a time. Use one technique for about a month, then add another.

I would love to hear from you and chat about your challenges, successes, and where you possibly need more ideas. Even if you only take away just one thing from this book – and use it – that will make a big, positive change in your family life and general sense of happiness. These positive feelings grow and can build on themselves, little by little, if you use the tips and techniques I will share with you.

I know you love your children enough to buy this book. I also know you want to make these small positive changes. I believe in you. I have seen parents change a behavior right before my eyes. The good parenting habits you develop now lay a foundation for... forever.

Chapter 1

Lead with Love

"Speak to your children as if they are the wisest, kindest, most beautiful, and magical humans on earth for what they believe is what they'll become."

—Brooke Hampton

It was late on a summer night. I had been woken from a sound sleep by the parents of the three small children I was babysitting. Yes, me... responsible for their safety, sound asleep in the recliner with the TV on. Startled, I jumped up, not a good ending to my first time babysitting, ever.

At age 18, I was getting ready to go away to college to major in music. My super nice neighbor had asked earlier in the week if I could watch her kids. *Sure,* I thought, *how hard could it be?* It was three little girls, the oldest about six, plus a set of three-year-old twins. The mother said she would keep me busy all summer watching her girls and I would have plenty of spending cash when I got to school.

After falling asleep on the job, it became my first and last time babysitting for that family, or actually any family for a couple years.

Looking back, I really didn't give it much thought. The job wasn't fun. The children were busy, messy, and didn't listen to me at all. No wonder I fell asleep – I was exhausted and bored.

Being the youngest of five kids, and having a mostly adult extended family, I had barely even seen a small child, let alone taken care of one. In the past, everyone had always taken care of me.

I was the last person you'd expect to change their major to Child and Family Development. But that's what happened when college music and living away from home turned out to not be a great fit. I decided to attend our local university. At the time, my older brother and his wife had a two-year-old child, and they regularly asked me to babysit while they went to Lamaze classes in preparation for their second child, or when they would go out for the evening.

This time I did not fall asleep!

I really enjoyed spending time with my nephew. I remember thinking, *Wow, he is an awesome little guy*. Later when his sister Chrystal was born, I watched her too. It was a bit more difficult with two children. My niece cried a lot but my nephew was so sweet and tried to comfort her. He kept telling her, in his little kid voice, "It's okay, Tistoy." He couldn't say her name. "It's Aunt Mona."

I loved hanging out with them. I began to think that little people were okay. I started looking into studying Child Development. After taking a few classes and loving what I was learning, I formally changed my major.

I told my sister I was going to be a preschool teacher. She said, "You won't make very much money," to which I replied, "I don't care. I'm going to change the world, one child at a time." Yes, I know. A bit dramatic, but I believed it.

Fast forward three decades, and big sister was right. She usually is. I do not make very much money. While I'm not sure if I have changed the world, I do know I have changed a few lives here and there. I also absolutely love my career. It gives me so much joy to watch my preschoolers grow and learn. Helping parents work through the difficulties and frustrations of raising small children is also rewarding. I do my best to make their lives a little easier by sharing my common-sense, experience-based wisdom and tips.

I teach differently, after raising and homeschooling four pretty great kids of my own. My philosophy has matured over the 30 years since I first decided that working with small humans could be just about the best job ever. I'm not saying it's easy. There have been plenty of children who have put me through my paces, tested and exhausted me. Yet, they have also inspired me to continue to learn, grow, and fill my bag of tools... to become a better teacher, and in turn mother.

I am in no way a perfect parent or teacher. I have a (wish-I-could) Do Over list just like everyone else, but if any of my experiences can help someone else and change a small part of someone's world, I want to try.

When I returned to the preschool classroom after homeschooling my children, I saw a lot of the "mean girl" thing happening. I remember the crisp fall morning in my class of three year olds when they were playing in the dramatic play area.

Jenny asked if she was allowed to play in the house. "Of course. Everyone is allowed to," was always my answer. Jenny told me sadly that Annie and Karen said she couldn't play there. "Go back," I replied. "I will watch you. Tell them the house is for everyone." I often use this technique to empower the child – letting her know she is right, and giving her the words. Then I watch to be sure it ends correctly. Jenny walked back to the dramatic play area and before she even said a word, Annie and Karen gave her a look, which Jenny knew meant "You can't play here." I walked over to let Annie and Karen know the house was for everyone and that Jenny could play in there and she didn't need to ask.

Later at group time, I felt a discussion was needed about being kind and what that meant. Now let me be clear, I'm not an everyone-has-to-play-with-everyone kind of teacher. It's not realistic. But when you say you don't want to play with someone, you have to be kind about it. I give children the words to help make that happen.

While discussing kindness, my brain jumped about ten years into the future. Scary, I know. I imagined these same children in High School and all of that drama. It played like a horror movie in my head. These sweet little people were already honing their "mean girl" bully skills.

Right then and there, my mind jumped back to the present moment and I said dramatically, with arms open wide, "Okay, put your listening ears on. This is a Miss Mona's advice for your whole life moment. *Don't play with people who are mean to you.* There are lots of friends out there. So pick a new one. In your whole life, only play with people who are kind to you!"

I hope when those children grow up, they will still hear these words in their heads and choose... wisely.

That is where it started. After that day, about once a month or so while reading a book to the students or observing something on the playground, it became a "Miss Mona's advice for your whole life" moment. I honestly couldn't help myself. In fact, I still can't.

Upon hearing some of these tips, many people said: "You need to write a book." It took a long time for that seed to sprout. I didn't feel entirely qualified. Yet others kept saying that young parents today would appreciate the tips I teach and help young students become happy, healthy, pleasant children.

> **Miss Mona's Advice for Your Whole Life:**
>
> *Don't play with people who are mean to you.*

I have my Bachelor's degree in Child and Family Development, but I don't have any other letters after my name. No M.A. or Ph.D. So, you can understand my reluctance to write a book. Yet as my husband told me, "You have been in the school of hard knocks for 30 years." Literally, at my first paying job, a four-year-old boy punched me in the nose.

As an imperfect parent of mostly adult children, and a teacher of preschoolers, I have a unique perspective – kind of like a giraffe. Giraffes have a long neck, so they're able to see the whole picture. I too can look back and see with a greater perspective... all the mistakes and possibly wrong choices, also the many good decisions made by the teacher (she existed first), then the wife and mom. I hope to share these experiences and knowledge to help make your parenting adventure a little easier.

Parenting is *messy*. It's good to laugh at the small stuff: spilled milk, fingerprints here and there, and skinned knees. It will all go by so quickly. My goal is to give you enough tips to make the exhausting, everyday challenges a little easier. The ultimate goal is to work yourself out of a job.

A mother of one of my preschoolers gave the best advice ever. She's a wise woman. *"I try to lead with love."* That's all you need to succeed. (Thank you, Stephanie.)

I wrote this book because I do want to change the world one child at a time, one family at a time. I hope to grow a lot more kindness in the world. It begins by parenting or teaching from that place in your heart, from kindness, love, and respect. I feel like our culture and our youth are missing a sense of respect. Respect for each other, themselves, and adults. When we parent and discipline our children it does not have to be mean or hurtful, but it does need to be consistent and come from a place that is love.

Here's to a joyful experience raising happy, healthy, children.

Chapter 2

The Perfect Parent (Not)

Toddler (n.) Emotionally unstable pint-sized dictator with the uncanny ability to know exactly how far to push you toward utter insanity before reverting to a loveable creature.

–Unknown

Let's face it: parenting is hard, and no one is perfect. It's just plain difficult!

You get tired and frustrated. When in public or with family and friends, your children have said or done something that embarrassed you. (Don't worry because the teenage years are ahead. Everything you do will embarrass them!)

Once I was at Costco when my daughter was about three years old. She stopped in the middle of the aisle, staring and pointing at the person coming toward us. Then my sweet, adorable, curly headed (cough, cough) child said, loudly, "Why is she so fat?" I honestly did not know what to say. I grimaced, mumbled, "Sorry," to the woman, then quickly moved through the store as fast as I could.

Can I say *Do Over* any louder?

I wish I would have apologized, better, then gently asked Maddie to apologize as well. Afterwards, off to the register with superhero speed. I wish I'd had a calm, loving discussion about being kind. Honestly, Madelynn was little, and she just didn't know her words might hurt someone's feelings. As parents it's our responsibility to teach them, lovingly. Because if we don't teach them, the world will. The world isn't always kind, nor is it necessarily the instructor you want teaching your child important life lessons and values.

There is no such thing as a perfect parent, so give that up right now.

I'm waiting for you to give it up.

Still waiting...

We all feel guilt and regret. We all want a second chance. My goal is to help you feel less of this. (Please ignore the teardrop stains on some the pages – this has been an emotional journey for me as well.)

In case you were wondering, there are no perfect children either. No, not even the neighbor's kids up the street who always appear to be well behaved, bathed and respectful at all times. They're really not.

You might need to remind yourself of this every day. I do. That's why I made this a separate, little chapter – so you can find it quickly and read it every day.

Now we can move on!

Why Do They Listen When You Say It?

Miss Mona's advice for perfect parenting

1. Always remember there are NO perfect parents.
2. There are no perfect children.
3. Always remember rule 1.

Chapter 3

1, 2, Cha-Cha-Cha:
Routines, Consistency & Follow Through

"Your greatest contribution to the world may not be something you do, but someone you raise." —Andy Stanley

---

I am not a dancer. Marching band was more my speed. However, both practices require the same thing – developing a routine. Do what you do, the same way every time. You will get good at it. It becomes a part of who you are, and it gets easier. Parenting can work the same way, as little people and life are often unpredictable.

Routines, consistency and follow through make it easier.

When our kids were little, we had a routine, albeit not a very good one. It was difficult to get things done and I rarely felt at peace. As our family grew and participated in more activities, I saw a need for a better way. I started getting up earlier and making an outline for the day. Then we started homeschooling and added another child to our family. I discovered early on if school didn't start by 9:00 A.M., we wouldn't have a very successful day.

The outline became a plan. I needed to be up and dressed before my kids got out of bed. I fixed breakfast and the kids got dressed, at the same time each day. When school started on time, they were happy... and so was I.

As they got older, I noticed they would go outside to play and run before school. This was life changing. My children taught me (yes, they teach us, too) that they could be more self-directed. I also discovered they had a much better school morning after running and playing. The afternoons were better, too. This routine made for a more peaceful school experience.

Remember there is no perfect.

Routines

Let's take a few minutes to talk about routines. They're a big part of being consistent.

There is comfort in our routines. Despite a bad reputation of being boring, they're not. They help us to know what comes next.

Even more importantly, routines can be life-saving for busy parents. In preschool we have a daily schedule. It's comforting for the children to know what comes next in their day. First thing when we come inside, we have a potty-turn, then next it's teacher activities, free-choice playtime, then group time, and finally outside time. I'm not saying we don't change it up sometimes – and they like that too – but when we do, we talk about it first.

Children are just like us but smaller and without a filter. In the same way you and I want to know what to expect, they like to know what is happening too.

We all imagine an idyllic, spontaneous life with our children, running in flower-filled meadows, pushing them on a swing in the park. It does sound lovely and there is time for all of it, but having a schedule for your days and weeks is helpful, both for us adults and for our children.

A daily schedule might look something like this:

- Get up (at the same time each day)
- Have breakfast
- Brush teeth
- Get dressed
- Playtime
- Story time
- Run errands
- Lunch
- Nap, etc.

Your week could look kind of like this:

- Monday—Stay home
- Tuesdays—Library
- Wednesday—Playdates at the park
- Thursday—Grocery store
- Friday—Parent time (Be sure to schedule this one. We often forget ourselves.)

Sometimes things interrupt our schedules. At school we have visitors or safety drills. We can we jump back in where we left off, or go on to the next thing. At home, necessary interruptions happen when we get sick, go on trips, or have plumbing problems. Interruptions are a part of the adventure of life.

Instead of getting stressed about the interruptions, talk to the plumber or washer repairman and ask them to tell your kids what they're fixing (however they will charge you more for this time). In my experience, most are happy to share. When interruptions are handled calmly usually everything goes smoothly. Children pick up on our moods and feelings, so if you stay calm usually they will too.

Some children do not handle change well at all. This is a subject for another time, but routines and our calm presence are even more important for these little friends. As with all things (I will say again and again), find the balance. When you can, please sing one more song, let them tell you the whole story about their painting, build one more Lego. These moments are priceless.

Consistency

Consistency is very important for everyone. As I said earlier, children need to know what to expect. When dealing with their behavior – especially negative behavior – we need to stay calm and deal rationally and consistently.

If you catch them coloring on the walls or cutting their little brother's hair, the best practice is to say their name followed by "freeze" or "stop!" You've gotten their attention.

Next, you need to consider a few things. First, how old are they? Do they need to just leave the area, or do they need time to think?

Your two year old usually just needs to leave the area or be redirected to a new activity. For very young children, the rule "out-of-sight, out-of-mind" can often resolve a simple problem. Redirection is showing or inviting your little one to a different toy or game.

> *If your child was coloring on the walls, get their attention and say, "We color on paper, not the walls," then move them and their crayons to the table with paper.*
>
> *When your child is coloring in the correct place, praise this behavior. "I like how you're coloring on the paper. That is helpful."*

Redirection also works well with ages three through five. These older ones can and should help to clean up their messes. If the behavior becomes a recurring thing, your child might need some "thinking time."

> *Thinking time is time away from an activity to sit and think. When sending children to a thinking spot, it's a good idea to remind them about making better choices. Thinking time is typically just a few minutes. Your child's age is the best measure for the number of minutes to spend in thinking time.*

If your child continues to make the wrong choices and is not listening when you ask them to behave, they need to completely leave the activity. It is usually for a longer amount of time, possibly 20–30 minutes. This isn't thinking time in a thinking spot, though. It's just away from the activity.

At four years and older, they know the rules and often feel the need to test them... and you. On occasion I have had to remove children from a play area or activity for the day. I really don't like to do this, and have only had to do it a few times with my big preschoolers, but sometimes little people are stubborn and don't believe what we say. Consistency helps children learn to believe us.

It is important that you be consistent when handling the same or similar situations. The best thing is to do it the same way every time. Children learn that when they do something they're not supposed to do, they will be met with a consequence.

When trying a new technique or consequence, stick with it. You need to give this new consequence a chance to be successful. Not every behavior modification technique will work for each child, but you do need to give it a fair amount of time. Some little people are stubborn, and if you haven't been consistent in the past, at first they may not believe you. Don't give up!

Follow Through

Do what you say you will do. Following through goes hand in hand with consistency. This is something we practice every day at preschool, but I learned fairly quickly that it is just as important at home. It also makes life easier.

If you're visiting with friends and your child takes a toy or hits, it's important to remind your child, "We use gentle hands." Depending on how old your child is, you may need to demonstrate what "gentle hands" means.

If it happens again, remind them again with a firmer voice and add, "You need to play gently, or you will not get to play."

To help them process the information ask, "How do we use our hands?" Hopefully, they will respond, "Gently." If it happens again – and sometimes it does – you will say, "I said that if this happened again, you would not get to play." Then remove them from the play area. Remind them again, "We play gently. There is no hitting. You hit your friend again, so now you cannot play for a little while." You will need to shift your child to another area with different toys.

Asking, "Why did you hit your friend?" can be helpful with verbal children. Usually they just don't know why. Instead ask, "Is there a problem? Is something wrong?" Maybe this friend was doing something to antagonize your child. Give the child space to answer. Then talk about using our words. Helping children to find the words to express how they are feeling is a valuable life skill. Empowering them to use their words is life-changing.

In the scenario above, everything you said was phrased in a positive way, spoken firmly but not harsh or yelling. You're not going to damage your child's self-esteem by moving them to a new play area or having them sit and think for 3–5 minutes. Your children need to learn and believe that you will do what you say you are going to do. With consistency and follow through, they will learn and know what to expect.

If you begin this when they are little, you will establish a foundation for your family and their whole childhood and teen years. You want your 16 year old to know their parents are "crazy" and will take the car keys and they'll be grounded "for the rest of their life" if they do *xyz*. That starts now while they are little. Eventually they will not need to test you. Or at least not as much.

For convenience sake, the children (who are not my own) used as examples in this book shall forever be named Kevin and Jenny. No, I have not had any misbehaving children named Kevin or Jenny.

Once on a beautiful, sunny, 75-degree day, my class of 15 preschoolers was playing happily outside on the playground. It happens, honestly, more often than you might think. I was with my teacher's aide on opposite ends of the yard. I was watching children build in the sand area. Then something disrupted the joyful laughter and squeals of the four-year-old group.

Jenny started crying, loudly. I bent down and asked her if she was okay. Still crying she said, "Kevin threw sand at me." I asked her to tell Kevin in her big outside voice, "Don't throw sand at me. I don't like it." She expressed herself very well.

Kevin is four years old and he knows that we don't throw sand. It's a rule he has heard before, so I sent him to play with Legos at the table. But soon, Kevin started throwing the Legos. This time Kevin and I talked a bit more about throwing things and what is okay and what is not.

I asked him, "What are we allowed to throw?" He answered, "Balls." Right! I told him, "It would be a good idea to go play ball on the other end of the yard."

Kevin played for a few minutes, then threw the ball really hard at a friend. Poor Kevin was having a difficult day.

I took care of the injured child first, then I told Kevin, "I think you need to take a break. Sit down and think for a few minutes."

After four minutes – based on his age – when his thinking time ended, Kevin and I talked about his behavior. He didn't really know why he was behaving the way he was, which is usually the case. Children have moods like we do, they just express them differently.

Kevin needed to learn to control himself. I explained to Kevin, "We have rules to keep all the children safe." I told him, "I do my best not to let anyone hurt you, and it is not okay for you to hurt others." This is something I see at school almost every day, but it translates well for home, too.

With Kevin, I tried redirection and eventually had to give him more thinking time – taking a break, or a time-out. What you choose to call it is fine. It's only a few minutes. But the thinking place needs to be boring. I used to send my kids to their room, but I learned quickly that was not boring. The stairs, however, were a much better spot at our house. At school it should be somewhere they can see everything, while I can see them.

Thinking time doesn't work for every child. If they won't stay in the thinking spot, you must engage more directly. I call it "being my partner." I don't talk to them until the partner time is up. I walk around the house or yard, doing what needs to get done, picking up toys, putting things away, all while holding their hand.

This is so *bo-o-o-ring!* Boring is exactly what is needed to get their attention.

If your child is older, sometimes taking away a toy or privilege works better. If they are having trouble making wise choices, tell them, "If you can't listen and make better choices, you will lose the chance to play with the toy or do that activity." If they still don't listen, you must follow through and take the toy or privilege away. Yes, even if they cry. If you are consistent and follow through every time, your child will learn to listen to your words.

Never say: "We will have to leave the park (party, store, etc.) if you don't listen," if you think you can't or won't follow through. **If you can't follow through with the consequences, do not say it**. If you do say it and you don't follow through, you will have just taught your child that your warnings don't mean anything.

Children learn quickly about who gives in and who doesn't. It's amazing to watch. Young children are smart – often smarter than we give them credit for. They learn to navigate and negotiate with the people around them. They're not bad little humans, it's just an innate survival skill.

Some children can do this better than others. Parents are children's first and primary teacher. It's our duty as parents to teach them and help them become healthy, happy, well behaved, social humans at home and out in the world. If we don't teach them, the world will and that is usually a more painful lesson. Honestly, I really don't want the world teaching my children.

Earn It Back

I believe in the idea of "earning it back." Earning a toy or a privilege back can be a good thing. It's positive reinforcement for the behavior you're helping your child to learn. Earning things back takes time, though. Your child needs to demonstrate they understand and can improve their behavior. If you needed to take away a toy or privilege, and then subsequently you see improvement, you can have a conversation like this one I had with my youngest son.

We had been a homeschooling family for many years. Michael, our youngest, was almost five years old, and adorable. At that point, he would do a little bit of school time, then he would get to play nearby while his older brother (whom Michael loved the most) and sisters would work on their schoolwork.

Michael discovered he was funny, and he loved making his older siblings laugh. To be completely honest, I had to work hard not to laugh myself and act more upset than I actually was, but it was becoming difficult for the older ones to get their work done.

I had tried sending Michael to the stairs for some thinking time. That was not much help for him. A couple of times I resorted to sending him to the corner, something I swore I would never do, and didn't like. Finally, getting frustrated, I decided to take away his basket of Legos (a most treasured item). This definitely got his attention, and kept it. When taking away a toy or privilege, it is important that the item is of high value to your child. After a couple of days, I had this conversation with him.

"Michael, I see you have been listening really well. Thank you. It's helpful, and everyone is able to get their schoolwork done on time. I still have your Legos, and I would really like to give you a chance to earn them back. If you continue to have listening ears, I will give them back to you."

I know several parents who have threatened and actually thrown toys away. If your child is having a very difficult time controlling their behavior, this can be an effective consequence – but only if you will actually throw the item away if it becomes necessary.

This consequence is for behaviors that have been continuous, where you have tried everything else, and you want the negative behavior to go away relatively quickly.

If you say the words, "I will throw away *xyz* if behavior *abc* happens again," if the behavior does not improve, you absolutely must follow through and throw the toy away. For those parents it worked. One parent I spoke with ended up throwing away a couple of toys.

However, if you don't follow through, you will lose credibility with your child. You will have taught them you don't follow through. Obviously, this toy cannot be earned back, and that's okay. *Do not* let your guilt drive you to Target to buy a new one. This needs to be a hard lesson to learn. Use it only for negative behaviors where other behavior modification techniques have not worked.

Miss Mona's advice
routines, consistency & follow through

1. Have routines in your day and week. They are comforting.
2. Be Consistent. Your children will learn what to expect from you and learn to behave (more often than not) accordingly.
3. Follow through. If you say it, you have to do it.
4. Earn it back. This teaches children they can learn to do better.

Chapter 4

Bite Your Tongue:
Communication Tips for Talking with Your Child

"Talk less... smile more."
—Lin-Manuel Miranda, *Hamilton*

We communicate in so many ways – the words we choose, the tone we say them with, our body language, even just a look. These can all convey an important message. With each of these different methods of communication we express happiness, disappointment, love, or even a "you need to do it now!"

With four children of my own, I have used all of these types of communication... daily, hourly, by the minute. The best advice, however, is to talk less and smile more.

I'll admit it, I use too many words. It's something I'm still working on. Even after 25 years of parenting and 30 years in a variety of teaching roles, I still have more to learn. It's also something my husband and I discuss because he's working on it, too. We can literally see our children shut down when one of us has verbally "thrown-up" at them. The thing you wanted them to hear is completely lost in all those words.

Tone of Voice

When your children are very young and words may not be completely understood yet, your tone of voice is most important. I often tell my own children and my preschoolers, "It's not what you said, it's how you said it." The same goes for us adults, too.

Try this. Say something as simple as, "It's time to clean up." Depending on how you say it, it will affect how others respond to you. If you say it in passing, when you're just walking through a room, you probably will not get any clean up. You'll end up frustrated and feel like no one is listening. Instead, say it directly, when you know you have your children's attention. Most likely, you will get some action while keeping everyone pretty happy.

What usually happens when we don't see results after the first or second request is that we now say it in a harsh tone, even angrily. The problem is, little people genuinely don't know why you're mad, and they begin to feel scared by your angry voice. Yes, you will probably get results, but it took longer and you end up feeling badly… and so does the child.

There's a big difference between your normal voice, your playful singsong voice, a firm tone, and a harsh angry voice. I have often talked with new teachers – as well as tired and stressed-out teachers – about the differences.

When teachers and parents are new, they often feel they should only speak in that sweet *singsong* voice. When things don't go as expected they don't understand why the kids aren't listening.

A tired, stressed-out teacher or parent can move quickly to the harsh side. I have experienced it myself. As teachers or parents, when we get too stressed we need a break.

A *normal* tone is just your conversational voice, which works great to get things accomplished. Just be sure you have their attention. Be sure they are looking at you, then have your child repeat what you said.

Firm tone is calm, not mean or yelling... but it's not conversational either. Children will hear the difference in the quality of your voice, so use a firm tone when your conversational voice did not get your desired results.

A *harsh* tone is both loud and mean, not at all conversational. It comes out when we're tired, overly frustrated, and need to take care of ourselves.

When talking with children, I speak in a regular conversational tone, like I would talk to you. Not the high-pitched, singsong tone you might think a preschool teacher would use. Maybe it's how you spoke to your child when they were an infant. This is commonly referred to as *motherese* or *baby talk*. Studies have shown that babies respond to this by smiling, and wiggling their arms and legs. It becomes a conversation.

Motherese is great for infants, because babies respond to it immediately. It promotes language development and helps them learn how conversations work.

However, it is not how we should be talking to our toddlers or preschool-age children.

When my tone changes, the child will understand something is up. If they don't notice this change in tone, I point it out to them. "Do you hear my voice?" Wait a few seconds for a response, then say, "I am not happy about *xyz*." Eventually they will learn to distinguish the different tones of your voice.

I just happened to be at McDonald's with my children (don't judge me), and my kids were playing in the climbing thing we lovingly refer to as the "Habitrail for Humans." It was a rainy day and we definitely needed to get out of our house. There were lots of kids happily playing, lots of chatter and laughter.

Then all of a sudden, we heard above all the other sounds of a busy fast food restaurant, "I don't wannnaaa goooo!" A boy about four years old cried out. All the other parents just kind of looked down at their phones feeling embarrassed and sorry for the child's dad.

Then I heard something even worse, like nails on a chalkboard to my ears. Thick and syrupy sweet, possibly cavity producing... "Come on, honey. It's time to go home." The man's son did not exit the building, let alone the Habitrail. "Daddy needs to get home. Come on." It went on for a while. When his son did, finally, come out of the Habitrail there was lots of negotiation. Eventually, the dad gave in and let the boy have three more minutes of playtime. When the three minutes were up there was still plenty of whining, stomping of feet, and protest from the child. They did eventually leave but it was exhausting to watch and it continued all the way out the door into the parking lot.

From a teacher's perspective, this was so interesting to observe. I completely understood, because I've seen similar situations plenty of times. Our children's behavior can be embarrassing and exhausting. As parents, we don't want to look like we are mean and terrible people. When we begin using clear language, along with consistency and follow through when children are little, we can avoid some of the frustration. But not all of it... because children test their boundaries. It's part of our human nature.

Children will also take clues from your body language. Before you say, "It's time to leave," it's a good idea to give your child a five-minute warning before you actually have to go. When the five minutes are up say, "It's time to go." Do not continue talking with your friends. It's confusing to your child if you say, "We're leaving," when you are not actually leaving. They will feel no need to leave either.

A helpful tip is that when you give the five-minute warning, set a timer on your phone so they can also hear it ring. When the timer goes off, you stand up and gather your things. Let them know the timer is ringing and it is time to go. For some children you may need to start walking toward the door, and usually they'll follow. If you try all of these and it still doesn't work (it happens), say in your firm voice, "Jenny, it's time to go. You can walk with me like a big kid, or you will have to hold my hand." Or "Jenny, it's time to go. You can walk with me like a big kid, or I can carry you to the car." Giving them the choice of walking or holding hands/carrying them empowers children. They learn to make the choice.

Raising your voice, or yelling, should be saved for matters of safety. Don't get me wrong... no one on this side of the page is claiming perfection. Far from it. I have definitely yelled at my own children, usually out of exhaustion and frustration. That's why self-care – the whole "put your oxygen mask on first" thing – is so important. But there have been moments I am not proud of when I yelled at my kids.

As a homeschooling mom I remember vividly yelling at my daughter, Maddie, because she was having trouble with her math. Truly, not my best moment, as I am still reminded about 13 years later. Madelynn had known how to do the math the day before, but the next day she couldn't figure it out. It's a real thing, although, at that time, I had no idea that could happen. Clearly, I needed a moment or ten. After I yelled, I apologized... and still do, to this day, when one of my kids reminds me (because they never forget).

At preschool I am much better at keeping calm. I've yelled a couple of times for safety purposes. The first involved a four-year-old girl and a hamster ball (those clear balls that small animals go inside to get some "fun" exercise). I can share this story because it has a happy ending.

It was late in the afternoon so only about 12 children were left at school with me and a teacher's aide. We were sitting on the floor between two groups of children. One group was playing a game, and the other had the hamster and were letting him run inside the ball in the middle of their group.

It was all going quite well, and everyone was happy… until I looked back and saw Jenny pick up the hamster ball, with the happy little hamster inside. She looked at the little critter inside, then lifted the ball over her head.

I yelled her name but not soon enough. Jenny chucked the ball across the room. It hit the floor, bounced and rolled and rolled. That poor hamster was pressed flat against the inside of the ball. It looked like something you might see in a cartoon. But he was tough, and he lived!

Afterward I spoke to Jenny calmly, and apologized for yelling. Then I told her, "We do not throw things inside. And we *never ever* throw animals." I used a firm tone and my facial expressions let her know what she had done was definitely not okay.

Of course, we never put the hamster in the ball again.

Years later, at another school, where our yard was located on a fairly busy street, it was after lunch and just before naptime. Five-year-old Kevin had decided he wanted to see his mom. He thought climbing the fence was the fastest and best way to get to her.

Several children had gone inside with a teacher to get ready for nap – last drinks of water, potty-turns – but the rest were outside with myself and one other teacher. These children were either waiting to go inside, or for their parents to pick them up.

I was facing the yard while my co-teacher was facing the classroom. Kevin was smart and typically a "busy" little guy, so when he walked to the corner of the yard, by himself, and really nothing was happening, I paid extra attention. When he put one foot on the chain link fence, I ran as fast as I could. When his arm reached up, I yelled as loud as possible, "Kevin, get down now!"

He was fast but I was faster. Adrenaline is a great thing. When Kevin and I both calmed down, we discussed what he had been doing and why. I explained that his mom needed him to be at school and safe, and she did not want him to climb the fence to go see her. I also explained that climbing the fence was not safe. Later, when his mom picked him up, I shared the day's events with her, and we discussed it together with Kevin. His mom was very helpful and understanding. He never did anything like that again. (*Phew!*)

Most of us have yelled at our children at some point. Frustration takes over and it happens, leaving us feeling badly. Give yourself a break literally and figuratively. When you become angry with your children (which you will) and you feel stressed (which you will), you need a break. If you cannot get a real break, tell your child, "I'm really upset right now, and I need a break." Then go to the kitchen to have a cup of tea (or better yet, dark chocolate). It is your own time out. Hopefully this is helpful.

If yelling has become your go-to method, or angry is your usual state of being, it might be time to take a parenting class or get some outside help. When parents hold unrealistic expectations about their children's behavior, problems can arise. Like in the story above about my daughter... one day she knew the math and the next day she didn't. I hadn't realized that could be a real thing. I thought she was being silly. I needed to talk with our homeschooling advisory teacher at the charter school about what was realistic. She was a great resource for our family.

Parenting is an around-the-clock task that no amount of training prepares us for. Learning happens on the job, which is why it is so important to talk to your parents, grandparents and friends with older children who have "been there & done that." These people have experience and valuable advice. Some you will use and some you will discard. Other people's experiences and advice (when asked for) is important, as you develop your parenting style and figure out what works for you.

The Words

Communication is important to every relationship. When you are communicating with a two to five year old, they do not need an entire Wikipedia page on why they shouldn't throw sand, or hit their friend, or knock down their brother's block tower.

This is where the talk-less-smile-more part comes in. Gesturing is good, too. Don't get me wrong... talking with your children every day is extremely important. Talking, reading and singing are how children develop language and learn how conversations work. But when you are trying to get a point across, less is more, especially when phrased in a positive way. Always tell them what they can do. For example say, "Sit in the chair, not on the table, please." Swap out "Don't run" for

"Use your walking feet" instead. Keep it short and sweet, because after too many words children tune us out.

When giving instructions, the fewer words the better. For example, say, "Kevin, put the Legos in the basket," or just "Legos go in the basket," with a gesture, pointing at the Legos then the basket. Honestly, you can start the practice of putting away toys very early, even before your child is a year old. It just requires your hand on theirs.

I watched this just the other day with a friend and her nine-month-old son. He had been playing with blocks on his tummy on the floor. When it was time to clean up she told him, with a cheery tone, "Time for put away." She sat him on her lap, held his hand in hers and they put the blocks in the basket together. She praised him every time they dropped a toy in the basket. It was beautiful, and will be helpful to them both as he gets older.

If your child has hurt someone, keep it simple. You don't need a lot of words. "Kevin, you hurt Jenny. That's not okay. How can you help her?"

It's very important to help the injured child first, asking Jenny what she needs, maybe a hug or an ice pack. Having the child who injured another help that child is also important. It makes the results of their actions very real.

I am often guilty of too many words (ask my kids). "Kevin, it is time to clean up now. Mommy needs to go to the grocery store before it gets too late." By the end of the sentence, poor Kevin has forgotten what you asked him to do.

Another example might be if your child is running through the house. Our first instinct is usually to yell, "Jenny, stop running in the house," but all she will hear is "running in the house," so... of course she runs more. A better way might be to calmly say, "Jenny, freeze." Now you have her attention. Then say, "Walking feet, please." This may not stop the behavior completely, but remember that she's little and excited, and it's easy to forget. You will have to remind, a lot.

Remember it's good to keep your sense of humor and to laugh (to yourself, though). Children are only little for a very short time. Being consistent will help them to remember. Loosely quoted from Dr. Ray Guarendi, "The more often you remind them, the less often you will have to." But you will feel better about calmly saying, "Walking feet," instead of yelling, "No running in the house."

At preschool this is a daily occurrence. You will often hear "Jenny, freeze" spoken in a normal conversational tone. Next I ask, "What am I going to say?" More often than not, the child will respond, "Walking feet," or "Use my walking feet." I give a big smile and reply, "I knew you knew!"

This creates a situation in which we both feel good about the outcome. If Jenny didn't know what I was going to say, I will often respond, "Look at your feet. What were they doing?" She will answer, "Running," to which I ask, "What do I need them to do?" I say it this way because it is my need, not hers. Most children will respond, "Walk." Then I close with, "Yes, thank you," and a big smile.

If the running continues you may need to say, calmly, "Jenny, I see you are having a hard time remembering to walk inside. Please choose something to do at the table or on the carpet."

When we use fewer words, we don't overwhelm our little ones with lots of information. Phrased in the positive, instead of beginning a sentence with "No" or "Don't" gives a concise, easy to understand message.

DON'T ASK

"Are you ready to go?"

"Are you ready to clean up?"

"Are you ready to go to bed?"

"Do you need to go potty?"

If it's not really a choice, *don't ask!*

My husband has told me several times that this was the first thing I taught him about raising our kids. It's something we all do without even thinking about it. In our adult brain, those questions mean the same thing as "It's time to go," "Clean up," or "Go to bed." We just think we are phrasing them more politely.

When our children answer these questions with a "No" or they just keep playing, we need to remember that they have heard you. You asked them if they were ready. They did listen, and gave you their honest answer.

I have done it myself and have seen it happen hundreds of times. But next time try this instead:

- *Give your child a five-minute warning that clean-up time is coming.*
- *When the minutes have ticked away say, "It's time to clean up now," or "I need you to clean up now."*
- *If they say no, then you can respond, "It's time to…"*

We all forget sometimes and phrase it as a question. When I forget and the child answers no, I often rephrase, "Oh, I'm sorry. I really didn't mean to ask you. I meant to say *it's time*."

When you say it without the question, what happens if the child says no or just doesn't answer at all and keeps playing? Say it again, firmly. If there is still no response (it happens), remember consistency and follow through. This is when you say, "I need you to clean up now. You can do it on your own like a big kid, or I can help you."

Usually, most children like to be the "big kid," but if not, you must follow through by holding your child's hand and walking with them from toy to toy, then put their hand on each toy, helping them put it in the basket.

If this becomes a regular thing, then you go to the next step, which is letting them know, "If I clean the toys, they will get put away in a box for a while." I have done this myself, at home and at school. I have even had parents tell me they have threatened to throw away toys, but this is a huge step, as we mentioned earlier. Remember… don't say it if you can't follow through!

Jenny Likes to Stay and Play

At the end of a long workday, a tired mother came into the preschool office to sign out her daughter. Jenny was playing with the office toys while her mom and I were talking.

When we were finished, mom said to Jenny, "Hey, are you ready to clean up and go?" Jenny kept playing and said, "No." The office toys were apparently very fun.

I gently said, "Jenny, your mom said it's time to go. I need you to listen and put away the toys." Jenny cleaned up.

The mother looked at me frustrated and asked, "Why does she listen when *you* say it?" (Hence the title of the book.)

I answered, "Because we say it differently." I felt badly about this. I try not to step in during parenting moments. Usually I speak with a parent out of earshot of the child or I involve the child in the conversation. But in this situation both mom and Jenny were tired, and I could see mom was really ready to go.

It's important to give our children choices as often as possible. It's empowering and teaches them their opinions are valuable. However, in real life, there is not always a choice – for adults or for children. The reason can sometimes be as simple as "I said so," or "There's not enough time," or for safety reasons. If there isn't a choice, it's easier and less confusing to children if we don't phrase our instructions as questions.

THE LOOK

One morning, my class of five year olds was out on the playground. Four girls laughed and played happily in the playhouse, making beautiful sand muffins, tacos, and pizza. They were completely unaware of the "danger" lurking right outside the playhouse window. Kevin stood silently, like a ninja, with his back pressed against the outside of the playhouse wall, holding a large sand scooper filled with sand. I could see the sneaky smile on his face.

"Kevin," I called, and gave him *the look*. He dropped the shovel and walked away.

Because I knew Kevin pretty well, I knew he was getting ready to do something he shouldn't do. And more importantly, he knew he shouldn't do it. That's why I gave him the look.

You've seen the look. Your mother or father gave you the look, and you knew exactly what it meant. You also have the power to use the look too. The skill comes standard with the parental package acquired at the birth of your first child.

After I got Kevin's attention, I looked him in the eyes. With my chin lowered, my eyebrows raised, and my lips pressed together, I followed with a slight shake of my head. More often than not, the undesirable activity stops, especially if your child knows you are consistent and will follow through.

Praise

Only a few words about praise, because it's pretty easy and we do it frequently. While it is important to praise children, if we do it all the time, it loses its potency. Like vegetables, if you eat too many you start to feel a little sick. But if you don't eat enough, you also start to feel a little sick. Finding balance is the key.

Thanking your children when they listen or help out around the house is great. Telling them why their actions are appreciated is even better. It's helpful for children to know *how* they've helped.

For example, "Thank you Jenny. You listened the first time. That's so helpful. Now we can get out to the park early."

When children proudly show you their artwork, try to tell them what it is you like about their drawings. Saying "I like the colors (or the shapes)" is more descriptive than "Oh, that's beautiful."

Too much praise for anything will make the praise lose its value. When I tell my children how wonderful they are for every little thing they do, it ceases to have meaning. They also become too dependent on outside approval instead of knowing inside themselves that they are enough... that their actions, drawings, or Lego structures are good.

Children want to do the right thing. Letting them know you're proud of them in the moment encourages that appropriate behavior. At preschool we sometimes give stickers for being able to sit still, or for participating at group time, or if they clean up well. But I don't believe in using tangible rewards all the time, as it's like verbal praise and it too will lose its value with overuse.

Sometimes we do things because we're supposed to or just out of the goodness of our hearts. I tell my own and my school children, "No one gives me stickers for washing the clothes or cooking dinner. I do it because I love my family." (Maybe we should get stickers for this behavior!)

However, when there isn't enough praise, children will look for approval everywhere... and that can lead to trouble as well.

Finding the balance might be difficult. How did your own parents do with you? Sometimes that is a good way to measure.

Miss Mona's advice — communication

1. Tone is important.
2. It's not always what you say. It's how you say it.
3. Don't ask if it is not a choice.
4. Keep it positive (when you can). Say what to do instead of what *not* to do.
5. A smile sends a positive message.
6. Praise, praise, praise, for doing the right thing... but find the balance.
7. Be consistent.
8. Follow through with what you say you will do.

Chapter 5

Flushing the Diaper:
Potty Training

"I have to do that??!!!" —Madelynn Smith

Her response after being told
she needed to try to wipe her bottom.

We won't actually flush the diaper, only your plumber will be happy about that!

"When should I begin potty training my child?" That is the million dollar question and there are many schools of thought on this subject.

Typically, children begin to and are capable of using the toilet around two years of age. That, however, is an average and some are definitely older. When your child shows interest in the toilet and in wearing underwear, that is an excellent time to start.

Here is the tricky part. Some children learn very quickly, some take longer, and others take *much* longer. Like with most things, everyone is different. If your child is not ready, it's usually us – the parents – who ends up potty trained until they *actually* get trained. This is one of those areas where they have us over the barrel, or toilet as it were. It's pretty much the last area where they have a major amount of control over their lives (and ours).

If you are planning to send your child to preschool, it's a good idea to check on their potty training/diaper policy, as children sometimes do need to be able to use the bathroom in order to attend.

If your child is interested in using the toilet, it makes it a lot easier, but if they aren't interested and are at that ideal age and are going to go to a preschool where they do need to be trained, I have some helpful tips that will hopefully make things easier for you and your little one.

In my own personal experience, girls often potty train earlier and faster than boys, and there's research to back it up. A study done at the Medical College of Wisconsin in 2002 proved it. In this study, girls showed interest in the toilet at 24 months while boys at 26 months of age, and girls stayed dry at 32 ½ months, while boys at an average of 35 months. These are not earth-shattering differences, it's just a trivial fact that may or may not be beneficial to you, and I like trivial facts.

I have four adult children that are all potty-trained proof it can be done. My children's names all begin with an M or a K, a girl and a boy with each letter. The "M" children learned to use the toilet very quickly and easily, the "K" children not so much.

Shortly, after Madelynn turned two, she told me she wanted to sit on the potty. Of course, I let her! While she sat, we chatted and I very sheepishly asked her, "Do you want to wear underwear?"

"Yes!" she answered enthusiastically from the toilet. We went and bought pretty panties that very day.

Never underestimate the power of cute or fun underwear for children.

Maddie was kind of amazing. She never had an accident or wet the bed. I did absolutely nothing – it was all her. I only responded to her request and praised her to the moon and back.

The boy "M" was similar, but he was closer to age three when he learned to use the toilet. He did have a few accidents but never wet the bed. I didn't have much to do with this one either.

The "K" children were a very different story. It took much longer and there were lots of potty accidents – at home, the grocery store, the dollar store, even a children's museum. You get the idea. Those two left their DNA almost everywhere we went. After tiring of changing and washing sheets, I began waking them up during the night and taking them to the bathroom before I went to bed. We also cut off liquids at 6:00 P.M. This was helpful, but not always. A friend of mine shared a genius idea to help handle nighttime bedwetting. When making your child's bed, use a mattress protector with a sheet over the top. Here is the genius part. Put another mattress protector and sheet on top of that. Brilliant, right? I wish I had heard of this 27 years ago.

Very important advice is don't give up the diapers until you are ready to deal with wet clothes. In the daytime, it's confusing to young children to switch back and forth from underwear to diapers, even with pull-ups. During the day it's a good idea to allow your children to experience wet clothes. They need to know what it feels like, and to have the disruption of their playtime while changing those wet clothes. When this happens, it's the perfect time to have a calm conversation while you're helping them get changed. Acknowledge what your child might be thinking and feeling, then let them know there is a better way. You could say something like, "I know it takes time to go to the potty, and you want to keep playing, but it takes much longer to change clothes and clean-up potty accidents, than it does to sit on the potty."

If your children are capable, let them dress themselves. This is a logical outcome, not a punishment. (Side note: they are usually more capable than we give them credit for.)

When they do make it to the toilet in time... praise, praise, praise! They need to know they did good, and using the toilet is something to be celebrated. Don't go crazy though. Stickers, Skittles, M&Ms or even a small toy are great rewards for using the toilet.

Our oldest child (a boy) took so long to learn to use the toilet that the first time he was successful, my husband was apparently so happy he bought him a giant Batman winged car thing. It was a bit much, but he was our first child after all, and it took a long time.

Night time is a different story. Staying dry at night takes longer to learn. Some children sleep so soundly they don't wake up when they need to go, or even when they are wet.

That was the case for my "K" children. They barely woke up even when their bed was wet. I chose not to use pull-ups, but looking back, I probably should have. This was my personal choice. I didn't work outside my home so I felt like I could sacrifice the sleep and try to catch a nap later. You should definitely do what is comfortable and works for your family.

We all do what we need to in order to make it through these early years. We need sleep. A sleep deprived parent is not a pretty sight. Taking care of yourself is important. If your child is at the age where they "should" be potty capable yet they are struggling, talk with your pediatrician just to be sure everything is okay.

For their whole life, your child has just gone potty whenever, without a thought. Gotta love a diaper. Using the toilet is such an odd concept unless you make it seem easy and interesting. It's one of the last places they have control of their lives, so when we step in and say it's time to use the potty, sometimes children can get a little stubborn.

A couple helpful hints:

Instead of asking your child, "Do you need to go potty?" tell them, "It's time for your potty turn." This was a life changing sentence that I learned pretty late in the game. I heard a teacher say it at preschool.

Saying "It's your turn" does not imply any kind of choice. When/if your child says, "I don't need to go," simply reply, "That's okay. Just try anyway. If nothing comes out, it's okay."

Be sure your child knows mom and dad have potty turns too. I can't tell you how many conversations I have had with my kids while I was on the toilet. Privacy pretty much goes out the window when you have small humans in the house.

My husband always says, "You need the right tool for the job. It makes everything easier." The same goes for potty training. For some children, using a grown-up sized toilet can be scary. A potty chair is a good idea, but if your child will use the big toilet, there are smaller toilet seats that can be attached directly to a conventional adult seat. This is a great invention that wasn't around when my kids were little. Your child won't have to wait for you to get the potty chair and there's no cleaning up the little potty chair (which is nice for you).

If your children choose the big toilet, they will need a step to help them get up. This is ideal, as your child learns to be independent, which is a great reward in itself.

Children do need help with cleaning themselves. Two year olds definitely need help. Young threes need some help too, while older three year olds may need to be wiped, and you let them try at the end. By age four, children should be starting to clean their own bottoms, especially when you send them off to preschool, but they may still need to be checked to be sure they are clean.

Preschool teachers do help children clean themselves. I have talked many a child through the wiping process. Not only do they get themselves clean, they learn they are capable, which is probably the best and most important reward of all.

Don't forget the hand washing. You need to teach that too! Wiping can be a messy process but teaching your child to clean themselves will build their confidence and independence.

Rewards can be very helpful in moving the potty-training process along. Some children need a little incentive, like stickers, Skittles, or M&Ms. "Behavior Modification" is the fancy Child Development phrase for this. Some call it bribery. It works.

How does it work? At first your child earns their (small) reward for just sitting on the toilet – one sticker or candy. When that becomes easy, they will actually need to go potty to earn the desired item. Remember, fun underwear often has amazing power! I used to remind my kids to try not to go potty on Spiderman or Cinderella (don't laugh, it works).

Pee and poop are different, obviously, as is your child's control of their bladder and bowels. Pee is definitely easier, and most often children learn this first. Controlling the bowels usually takes more time. You may even find your child has a "time of day" that they go poop, If you find this is the case for your child, it would be a good idea to say, "It's your potty turn," at that time of day.

Sometimes children hide or touch their bottoms when they need to go, but if asked, "Do you need to go?" they will usually say no. If you notice this happening, it's time for a conversation, telling them, "When you touch your bottom or hide, and then go potty in your pants, you need to tell Mom or Dad that you need to go potty, or just run to the bathroom, and then yell for someone to help you."

More proficiency in the bathroom will increase your child's feelings of capability and independence. After all your ultimate goal is a happy, self-reliant human.

Miss Mona's advice
potty training

1. Potty training is a process. Be sure you and your child are ready.
2. Have the right tools for the job.
3. Once you start the toilet training process, don't ask your child if they need to go. Simply say, "It's your potty turn."
4. It's a good idea to let your child know you take potty turns too.
5. Rewards can be helpful and sometimes needed.
6. Be patient—it's a process.
7. Keep your sense of humor!

Chapter 6

Preschool or Not:
Sometimes It Is a Fact of Life

"Play is often talked about as if it were a relief from serious learning. But for children play is serious learning. Play is really the work of childhood."

—Mr. Rogers

Your child is two, three, or four years old and everyone else is going to preschool of some kind or another. Time has flown by so fast that you haven't even considered it yet. That's okay.

If you know you want to send your child to preschool, or you will eventually need to go back to work, you really should start looking now. If you are pregnant and know you will need infant care, begin your search even before baby arrives. I can't tell you how many calls I have received from parents who waited too long. You'll feel more comfortable if you have choices.

Food for thought: When you do find your ideal school, if you are offered a space for your three-year-old, but you are waiting until your child is four to send them to school, you might want to take that earlier spot because you will likely have a better chance of getting your child into your preferred school.

If you choose not to go to preschool, that's great too. Home is wonderful! Where we lived when my kids were little I didn't care for my preschool choices, so my kids didn't go. I did have to return to work for a short time when my oldest was two. The school allowed teachers' children to attend so Kyle went with me and was in my class because it worked for my family.

If you aren't sure whether you want to send your child to preschool, talk it over with your partner or someone you trust and whose opinion you value. Preschool is a personal choice. If you can afford to be at home and it is a life you would enjoy, and you have ways of giving your child and yourself social experiences, it's a great option.

I was home with my four kids for about seventeen years. Being a stay-at-home mom is not what I thought I wanted. But when it happened, pretty much by accident, I loved it. If you can, I honestly believe you will not regret being home with your children. However, it doesn't have to be an all or nothing situation. Most preschools have a half-day program. This way you get the best of both worlds – home and school.

If you are choosing to stay home, playgroups and Mommy & Me programs are an excellent way for you and your child to make friends, which is very important. You need friends just as much as your children do. Learning to share and take turns are important concepts but it doesn't necessarily have to happen in a classroom.

If you are choosing preschool, great. There are so many different types to choose from, so it will be important to find the right fit for your child and family. This decision leads to a plethora of questions.

CHOOSING A PRESCHOOL/CHILDCARE

There are many different types of philosophies. Do you want a school near your home or work? Should the philosophy be: play based, Montessori, religious, or a parent cooperative, or a home daycare? This is most definitely not a complete list, but it gets you started. Each type of philosophy has its own pros and cons. How closely they adhere to the philosophy may affect how you feel about each program.

Choosing a school can be overwhelming. The key is to start early and ask friends and family where their children went. Visit schools, then visit a few more. If you can, it might be best to have your little one stay with a friend. Touring many sites is tiring and can be confusing to your little one, so if possible, have your child stay with a friend until you narrow down your choices. Then when you have a couple you really like, if needed, tour again with your child. Be sure to explain to your child, "We're just visiting to see how we like the school." I have seen many children get upset when it's time to leave.

While you're touring the schools ask questions... lots of questions! What questions? That is a good question.

Please don't feel like any question you have is a stupid question. I'm sure you have your own list but here are a few I would ask:

1) *Are you licensed?* I prefer a licensed school, as licensed means the school has been inspected by Community Care Licensing or the Department of Social

Services and is deemed safe. I like it that licensed schools have a surprise visit from the licensing agency every year. As a teacher it can be a bit unnerving, but if you're doing all the right things, it's fine. It's kind of like when a police officer is following you and you know you're driving well, but you still feel nervous. If a school has any deficiencies, they are written up and the form must be posted at the school for parents to see. The licensing agent will return later in the year to check on the school's progress for improving the deficiency. You can also get the school's license number and call your local Community Care Licensing office and check them out.

2) *What is the school's philosophy?* There are many to choose from.

3) *What is your teacher-to-child ratio?* I live in California where the ratio for preschool age children is 12:1. That is twelve children to one teacher. For toddlers it is 8:1.

4) *How do you handle discipline?* The answer to this question will give you a lot of information about the school.

5) *My child is sensitive, busy or xyz. How do you handle that?*

6) *Does my child need to be potty trained?*

7) *Is nap time a requirement?* It's not at every school.

8) *How much outside time do the children have?* Outside time, being in nature, is something many schools are shrinking. It is hugely important to have

plenty of time outdoors. There is so much to learn while playing in sand, water, or while riding bikes.

9) *Am I allowed to visit the classroom?* You should be. How much time, or whether or not you actually should, is a topic for another time.

10) *Is the school accredited?* The National Association for the Education of Young Children (NAEYC) has requirements that hold accredited schools to a higher standard.

While the center's Director or Assistant Director is giving you a tour of the school, at least some of your questions should be answered before you even ask them. You should get a general feeling about the center, meet some of the teachers, and see active, mostly happy children. If you see a child misbehaving, bonus! Watch and listen to how the teachers handle the situation.

Pay attention to how the teachers talk with the children in general. Look around the classrooms. Do you like what you see? Does the art on the walls look like preschool art – like the children completed it themselves? It should not be perfect or all look exactly the same. Most importantly ask yourself if you feel comfortable in the center. If not, it's probably not the right fit, even if it is the most popular school in your area.

Children are very intuitive; they pick up on our feelings. Typically, if we like something and are comfortable, our children will follow suit. If you love the school, most likely your child will too.

There may still be an adjustment period when you start. Some tears or clingy behavior is definitely the normal range. But most children adjust very quickly. If your child is having difficulty, ask their teacher for suggestions. After all, they are there to help you.

Choosing the right school for your child and family makes all the difference in the world. Pay attention to your inner voice. Parent radar is a good thing.

> **RED FLAGS**
>
> 1. The school is not licensed.
> 2. The school will not allow you to visit, or you can only come at a certain time of day (after your child is enrolled).
> 3. The school is not clean. I don't mean sterile, just not taken care of like you would at home.

> ## Miss Mona's
> —— advice ——
> choosing a preschool
>
> 1. Get referrals from friends & family.
> 2. Visit several schools.
> 3. Ask lots of questions.
> 4. If you like a school and feel comfortable, chances are your child will too.

Chapter 7

No More Static Cling:
Separation Anxiety Tips for an Easier Goodbye

See ya later, alligator.
After while, crocodile.
Out the door, dinosaur.
Toodle-loo, kangaroo.
See ya soon, raccoon.
Bye bye, butterfly.

Whether you're sending your child to preschool or not, you will eventually entrust your child to the care of someone other than you, your partner, or a grandparent... eventually.

With our first child, we didn't have family nearby. We did have a good friend, but she had a child the same age as ours. I honestly couldn't see how she could take care of my child and hers at the same time. Let's chalk that up to new-mom brain.

So, Kyle went everywhere with us, or Dad stayed with him while I ran errands. Luckily for us, Kyle was what we lovingly referred to as a portable baby. We really could take him anywhere. When we did finally go out, just the two of us, a very trusted friend from my preschool was his first babysitter. Linda was in her 40s and had three big kids of her own, but of course, I also asked another younger teacher for backup. We would be gone for at least three whole hours. How could one person watch my infant child for three hours all by herself (I ask very sarcastically)? After all he was only six months old.

It was obvious I was nervous to leave my child for the first time. Everything went great, and it definitely got easier from there. Don't follow my example here, because six months is probably too long to wait to go out.

At home with a babysitter, at Grandma's house, or preschool, separation is the time when you say goodbye to your child. Sometimes it's easy, but other times not so much. Some of those difficult times I've actually referred to as being like childbirth. It can be painful. Separation anxiety is real and it goes both ways. We know our children sometimes feel it, but parents can feel it too.

How you handle the goodbye directly affects how your child will handle it.

After the caregiver has been carefully chosen, and you're preparing for your child's first day away from you, you're probably feeling a wide range of emotions – excited, sad, guilty, maybe all of the above plus possibly even angry. Perhaps you wanted to stay home and for many reasons that's not possible.

You might think you're crazy. Welcome to parenthood. These and many other emotions are all normal feelings. Whatever it is you feel there are some simple steps to help make it easier for both parent and child.

As adults, when going into a new situation, we usually like to have an idea of what we're walking into. I know I do. Children really aren't much different than us, just smaller. Talk to your child about where they are going, and where you'll be all day. Hopefully, you have introduced your child to their caregiver and shown them the building ahead of time. In the days leading up to their first day of childcare, remind your child who will be there, how long they'll be staying, and when you'll be back to pick them up. Even if they're an infant, start the routine now. Remember to keep it light and fun! Our children feel what we feel. If you are sad about leaving, you have to suck that up and be happy for your child.

If your childcare is outside your home, plan to send a bit of home with your child.

A few ideas:

- Extra clothes (labeled with your child's name)
- A small lovey (stuffed animal or blankie)
- If you need to provide a lunch, let your child choose the lunchbox.
- If there will be a naptime, allow your child to choose the blanket.

All of this comfort is important when you and your child are transitioning into a new situation. It is also comforting for your child to know when they will be going home. Your child will get used to the time you "normally" pick them up – after nap or snack, before Kevin goes home, or just after Jenny leaves. These time markers help children to know what happens next.

Young children... well, most young children... can't read a clock – but they can *tell* time. Their body clock is very accurate. In my class, we sometimes stay outside longer when it's a lovely day. When we do, at least one child will ask, at the correct time, "Is it time to line up?" They definitely can feel time.

This is why it is important to try to pick up your child at the usual time. Things happen and sometimes we are late and that's OK. If you will be late, call the school or sitter and let them know. Ask them to tell your child. We do this all the time at my school. The children are able to enjoy their extra play time this way.

When it comes time for the actual goodbye, sometimes it will be easy, and sometimes terrible. Miss Mona's Advice for Your Whole Life is to always expect the best, but be prepared for the worst.

When you do say goodbye, it should be like ripping off a bandage. Ouch? Not if you do it quickly. When you pull a bandage off slowly, it takes longer and there is more pain. Do it quickly and it's over and done with. You both move on to the next part of your day.

If it is difficult for you or your child, no matter how painful... you must *always* say goodbye. There is no sneaking out, not even at home when Grandma or the favorite babysitter is there and ready to make mac and cheese.

"Why?" you ask. My mom used to say to my husband and me, "Oh honey, just sneak out, it's okay. I don't want him to cry." But when you sneak out, your child thinks you've disappeared, especially if they are very young. That would be scary for anyone. When you say goodbye and tell them what time you'll be back, you develop a bond of trust, and they will feel more secure.

It's good to set this example now, because when they're older, you'll want your teenager to say goodbye to you when they leave the house.

Every day at preschool I watch parents say goodbye to their children. Most separations are easy, and some are so pain free I actually have to remind the child to say goodbye and I love you... "Because Moms and Dads need that stuff."

If your child separates easily, but you feel some anxiety, do not stay longer or prolong the goodbye until your child begins to cry. This happens more often than you might think. There are times we feel like our children don't need us (honestly, they sometimes don't). This is a good thing. Remember we are working ourselves out of the job. It will be okay. This is a process and it takes time. I promise they do still need you. Even when they're grown they will still need you – sometimes.

If your child is separating easily, it tells you they are confident and trust you will come back when you say you will. Let's look at this as a positive. If your child doesn't have separation issues, do not give them yours.

There are those times when I refer to a separation moment as *childbirth* because it's so painful to watch. When I feel like the parent is ready for an easy goodbye, sometimes it can take a week or two for the parent to realize that the extended goodbye is exhausting and isn't a positive way to start the day. This is when I step in. Ultimately, the parent needs to be ready.

I once had a student, Jenny, who every day would come into the classroom and put her things in her cubby. Mom would sit down with Jenny for a few minutes then say she needed to go. She'd give Jenny a hug and a kiss, and then Jenny would cry and hang onto her mom's leg. The mother would kneel down, hug Jenny, and say, "Okay, one more minute."

When the mother would again stand up to leave, Jenny would cry. I stepped in and said, "Jenny, I'll hold you and we'll read a book while mom goes." Typically, I needed to actually pry Jenny, still crying, off of mom's leg. This wasn't pleasant for any of us. It wasn't easy either. Little people are strong.

Once I removed the suction cup like grip, I would hold Jenny gently by her shoulders and walk her to the library area to choose a book. After a minute or two she was happy and ready to play with her friends.

It could have been so much easier for all of us. After a couple weeks of this painful pattern, I finally asked mom, "Do you want to know the secret to an easy goodbye?"

"Yes, please," she answered quickly. "You and Jenny need to have a plan." The routine needs to be the same each day. It should look something like: arrive at school, she puts her things in the cubby, then the parent asks what activity she is going to start with this morning (play dough, painting, or play with friends, etc.), then one hug and two kisses goodbye. Tell her the time you'll come back to pick her up (after lunch, during outside time, etc.). Your plan should be short and sweet, like ripping off a bandage. If you do it too slowly it will only hurt worse, but pulling it quickly is easier and much less painful in the end.

Jenny and her mom came to school the next day ready with a goodbye plan. It worked! Mom was amazing, calm and guilt free. Jenny was actually smiling when her mother left.

Having a plan allows for a much better start to the day, for everyone. There will still be those days when your child won't want to go to school (we all have those days). If your child does have occasional setbacks, allow the teacher/caregiver to do their job, which is helping your child to get comfortable with you leaving.

A parent at my preschool had an awesome morning drop-off routine. Each day, when the mother walked into the classroom, she would ask her son, "Do you want to go with Miss Mona, or do you want to play with friends?" Sometimes he would choose me, and we would find a game or a book. More often than not he would choose friends. She would give him a kiss and leave. It was wonderful and so empowering for her son. Anytime we can give our children control over decisions, it builds their self-esteem, encourages independence and is generally better for everyone. We all want to have a "say" in what happens to us.

I've seen this method – having a plan – work more times than I can count. One morning I actually overheard a mom telling her husband, who was new to dropping off and was having a difficult time with their son's goodbye, say, "You just have to do it. It's amazing!"

While I have seen this technique work on the first time, there are still those children who need a little more proof that you mean what you say. If you've had trouble being consistent and following through in the past, this may be the case for you. Let your child's teacher help you and don't give up. It's in everyone's best interest to help your child through this phase. A pleasant, easy goodbye is life changing.

Saying goodbye at home, school, a grandparent's house, or the babysitter's can be difficult. Remember you are your child's first source of comfort and safety. That being said, it's still okay to leave your child in someone else's care. Teaching our children they are safe and cared for with someone other than mom or dad, is an absolute necessity.

Side note: Whether at home or preschool, if you've forgotten something inside, *do not* run back to grab it. Instead, call your caregiver and have them place the item outside. If you go back inside the separation process begins again.

Miss Mona's advice — separation

1. Always say goodbye, no sneaking out. Children will learn to trust and feel safe with others.

2. Keep it short and sweet—like ripping off a bandage. Give a kiss and a hug. If there are tears, allow your caregiver to do their job and help your child through.

3. Do not go back inside. If you've forgotten something, call your caregiver and have them put it outside. The whole process begins again if you go back in.

4. Be on time. If you will be late for pickup, call the school so they can tell your child. Most young children can't tell time, but they can TELL the time. Preschool-age children have a great bodily clock.

Chapter 8

Tantrums, Swearing, and Fighting, OH MY!!!

"When little people are overwhelmed by big emotions, it's our job to share our calm, not to join their chaos."

—L.R. Knost

TANTRUMS

Oh my, is right. Tantrums, swearing, and fighting are the biggies for the 2–5 year-old set. It's probably a good idea to throw biting in there too. As parents we hope to avoid these episodes altogether, but that's probably not going to happen. It's best to just relax and deal with them calmly and rationally.

If you miss out on one or the other, don't feel deprived. Chances are good, if you have children, then you will eventually experience at least one – if not all – of these behaviors.

Realizing these behaviors are common for young children, and knowing in advance how you want to handle them before you see them will put you ahead of the game. If you're like me and thought your child would never bite or have tantrums, think again. None of us are immune.

Usually these are things you will laugh about later, after your children are grown. When my third child, Kaylee, was almost two years old, she learned a great new trick, or so her big brother thought. She began having temper tantrums – kicking, screaming, throwing herself on the floor, and hitting her head. As a teacher and a parent, I believed this was a learned behavior. They see it and they try it out, but Kaylee had not seen anyone having a tantrum before.

I can vividly remember the first time it happened. We lived in a two-story house. I blocked the stairs so Kaylee couldn't go up alone. Although she wanted to all the time, she wasn't able to navigate them very well yet on her own. My son Kyle (who was eight) and Maddie (about four) could and did, often. *Oh, the injustice of it all!*

That baby gate was for Kaylee's safety. She would sit at the bottom and watch her siblings go up and down. When she tried, I told her no.

You can probably imagine what happened next. First there was the blood-curdling scream. I'm pretty sure it was heard in the next county. Then she threw her head back, hitting it hard on the tile floor, which must have been quite painful as it was followed by more, really loud screaming that lasted for what seemed like forever.

Neither of my older two had ever done this. The three of us watched in amazement. Then Kyle and Maddie started laughing hysterically – which only made Kaylee scream more.

When it was over my son said, "Mom, make her do it again and I'll film it."

"No, I'm not going to make her do it again." Because really, who would want to ever see that again? It was awful and a little scary.

Apparently, I didn't have to make her do it again. Tantrums became a regular occurrence in our home, not just about the stairs, but pretty much anything that limited her exploration. I told my husband we should probably buy her a helmet so she wouldn't suffer brain damage.

Honestly, I don't remember how long this period of tantrums lasted, but it was exhausting. One morning after a truly terrible tantrum, I sat on the floor with her on my lap. I was crying, asking God, "What do I do with this girl?" If you are a praying person, I highly recommend it. Eighteen years later, Kaylee did not damage her brain! She grew out of the tantrums and found using words was more efficient. Turns out she is now big on journaling, a prolific writer of stories and music, with an amazing vocabulary. You really don't want to debate with this young woman!

Typically, temper tantrums consist of crying, kicking, screaming, hitting, and throwing themselves on the floor. They are more common for two year olds because the younger child's vocabulary is limited. They simply don't have as many words as they have thoughts. They can't express themselves in a way that the adults in their lives can understand their wants and needs.

Children get frustrated, just like us, when they aren't understood. Often, they can't tell you exactly what they want or how they feel. Tantrums are their way of expressing themselves, albeit inappropriately.

Tantrums can be scary for the child and the observer. As parents we really just want it to end. (The sooner the better, right?) This often means we give the child what they want... but as a result, our children learn this is how to get what they want. Rewarding the tantrum, or any negative behavior, pretty much guarantees it will happen again, which is probably not your desired outcome.

So, what can we do?

Everyone wants some control or power over their lives, even your two-year-old child. When you can, avoid the tantrum altogether. You may know or will soon learn what sets one off. Now I don't want you walking on eggshells around your child because that's not healthy for anyone, but when possible, try not to run errands when your child is tired or sick.

Sometimes you can test out every bit of good parenting advice, yet your child still has a tantrum. It happens. In these moments, trying to talk them down usually only makes it worse. Sometimes you just have to let them have their tantrum in a safe place where they won't hurt themselves or others. It's okay to busy yourself with something else, or walk away. When you say to your child, "We can talk when you're calm," you might be surprised how quickly the tantrum ends without an audience. However, don't go too far away... just out of sight will do. You still want to be sure they're safe. Then as the tantrum ends, hold your child, rock them calmly, and remind them to breathe slowly, demonstrating calm breathing for them.

Your 3–5-year-old child may start having tantrums, though not as common. If there are changes at home – new babies, new jobs, different schedules – these changes can cause your child to worry, and the only way of expression your child may know is tantrums.

If you have an idea of why your child is upset that is often helpful. There are different types of tantrums and they serve different purposes. But no matter what, even if your child is worried about the changes happening around them, you can't give in to a tantrum. When they're calm and quiet you can talk with your child about how they're feeling. They might need more hugs and reassurance that everything is okay.

Ask yourself, "Is my child looking for control?"

For example: If your child is kicking and screaming, "I don't want to go to bed. I want to watch TV with you," then try saying something like, "I wanted to do that too, but you're having a fit so we can't right now. If you can calm yourself down, brush your teeth, and put on your pajamas, we can watch your special show tomorrow." In doing this, your child will begin to learn they can calm themselves and follow directions... and they will get the thing they want – just not right now. It's a win-win.

Your child may have a tantrum because they're feeling helpless. If this is the case your child is looking for empowerment, basically wanting to have a say in their life. When you can, and as often as you can, allow them to have choices such as their clothing, which park to go to, or which fruit or vegetable to have with their lunch.

These aren't difficult to implement, and in the process you will help your child learn to make good choices, which is an excellent life skill.

If the tantrum happens in a store, birthday party, or public place, we don't need to torture the entire gathering of people. You will need to pick up your screaming child and leave immediately. Place them in the car, then go home and send them to their room or other quiet spot for two to five minutes (depending on their age). When they've calmed down, then you can discuss the tantrum behavior, and explain that you can't give them that thing they really wanted when they're yelling at you. They need to use their calm words.

Next, ask them to tell you how they do get things they want. Hopefully they will say something like, "By using nice words." The next time you go to that place where the tantrum occurred, it's a good idea to have a conversation about what happened the last time. Let the child tell you. Then ask them how today is going to be better. Again, let them tell you. Allowing your child to tell you helps them process the information, internalizing it and becoming better prepared if the same tantrum triggers come up again.

I'm not saying they won't have a tantrum ever again. This will take some time, practice, and growth. When your child learns they can control themselves, use their words and make choices (within reason), the intrinsic reward of this will make them feel like a big kid and good about themselves... which is necessary for healthy, happy children, and is ultimately what we're all working toward.

Miss Mona's advice — tantrum tips

1. Do not give in. Children learn quickly what works, and who's easy... and they repeat the behavior.
2. Don't have a conversation with the child during the tantrum. Trying to explain why they can't do or have something prolongs the tantrum. Only say, "I will talk to you when you're calm."
3. Redirect children from their tantrum triggers, before the tantrum happens.
4. Choose your battles. Spontaneity is good. When you can, give choices: "Do you want carrots or broccoli with dinner?" "Do you want to wear the blue or the red shirt today?"
5. Reinforce positive behavior.

SWEARING

I bet you would never expect to hear your cherubic, angel faced, four year old cursing like a sailor when they've dropped their toast, butter side down, on the kitchen floor. (No disrespect to sailors, because my dad and father-in-law were both sailors and wonderful men.) You hear, "Oh, s#&*!" After you catch your breath, pick up your jaw off the floor and stifle a laugh, how do you respond to your child?

Imagine the following situation. After a long day at work you go to pick up your child at preschool where you are intercepted by your child's preschool teacher, who relates this story to you with a slight smirk on her face. "Today, Kevin and a friend were driving trucks around the yard. While stuck in preschool dumptruck traffic Kevin yelled, *'F%$#, Jason. Go faster!'*" In this instance, the dad fessed up rather quickly. He smiled sheepishly and said, "It's me. I'm sorry, I'll fix it."

Your first reaction might be to laugh, but try not to – at least in front of your child. It can be funny, especially if they use the word in the correct context and tone. You may wonder how your precious little one learned to talk like that. This can be *relatively* (pun intended) easy to figure out, but not so easy to fix because you might have to change your own behavior first, or that of a family member, which can be the hardest part.

Typically, at preschool the "bad" words we hear most often are *stupid*, *poop*, and *butt*, though we do hear the more adult versions of these words on occasion. How we handle the situation depends on the child's age and the frequency of the usage. With a two year old, ignoring and eliminating the word from their surroundings will usually do the trick. For the older ones, we usually ask, "Is that a word we use at school?" or "Do you say that in front of your mom (or grandma)?" They always answer no with wide eyes. Sometimes that's enough to take care of the behavior.

Kevin's Story

One year in my 4–5-year-old class, Kevin was using potty words, of all sorts, at home and at school. His mom and I had talked about it quite a bit. It was becoming a daily occurrence, and other parents began telling me their children were using bad words at home and saying they learned it from someone at school.

Of course we always kept names private, but I did assure the parents that we were working on this with the family, and they were concerned too. We would be talking about it at group time as well.

Kevin's parents had tried everything and didn't know what to do. I suggested they try taking away a privilege. Kevin's parents are excellent at follow through, so I thought this might work.

The next day at school, Kevin told us if he used potty words he wouldn't get to go to a birthday party. We always try to help children remember to do the right thing so we gave Kevin a few reminders during the rest of the week.

Unfortunately, Kevin was not successful – a few times. Each day his mom or dad would ask at pick-up how he'd done that day. I was sad to report Kevin had used potty words. They told him he would not get to go to the birthday party that weekend.

I had a private conversation with Kevin's mom. I said, "I know this is going to sound really mean, but if you don't go to the party, Kevin won't know it even happened. He won't remember. It might be a good idea to get the birthday gift, wrap it, and take it to the party, but just drop it off and leave. He needs to know he's missing it." That is exactly what they did. We never heard potty talk from Kevin again.

If reminders don't help and the words have become a habit, you will need to be more proactive. You don't want your little one teaching the whole preschool or neighborhood how to swear. At first, you might consider an apology to your child. "Kevin, Mrs. Teacher told me you are saying potty (bad) words at school. I need to say I'm sorry to you, because I have been saying bad words and it's not okay. If you say them, you will get in trouble, so we are both not going to say them anymore." Shake hands, fist bump, pinky promise, whatever it is to help you both to agree to stop. If you need reminders, be sure your child knows it's okay to remind you. Maybe instituting a swear jar would be helpful. For your child, if the swearing doesn't go away, they may need to lose a privilege or a toy if they have a difficult time of it.

Good luck and remember nobody is perfect.

Miss Mona's advice
swearing strategy

1. Try not to laugh.
2. Stop swearing yourself and ask those around your children to stop swearing.
3. Ignore the swearing. It may go away on its own.
4. If swearing doesn't go away, be proactive.
5. Remember to be consistent and follow through.

FIGHTING

Believe it or not, young children do occasionally hit each other. Then they tell on each other. The typical 2–5 year old learns quickly that hitting is often a quick fix to a common problem: *you have it, I want it!*

It happens a couple of different ways:

- You have it, I take it, you hit me, I tell on you for hitting me.
- Hit first then grab the toy.

At preschool, we work on the social and emotional aspect of this. We do not allow hitting. We encourage and facilitate the use of words. When someone gets hit, we help them to tell the other child something like, *"Don't hit me. I don't like it when you hit me."*

We then ask the injured child if they need anything – an ice pack, a hug, or an apology. Miss Mona also tells them they need to say it really loudly. This way everyone looks and sees what is happening. We also ask the injured child if they need anything from the child who hit them. And let them know they do not have to say "please" when telling someone not to hit them.

These ideas work well at home too.

For some situations, how things are handled between home and school can be different. At school, we don't make the child say they're sorry (unless the injured child needs an apology). Why not? Typically the other child isn't sorry. Nor do I ask why they hit, as they usually don't know. Older children do sometimes know exactly why and will tell you so, which leads to a very interesting conversation. If the child has been hitting or having a difficult time listening, tell them, "Find somewhere else to play. Or do you need some time to think and regroup while sitting by yourself?"

At home as a parent, when my kids would hurt each other, I did make them apologize. "Sometimes we own a word before we own a feeling." Boy, I wish I had said that first, but it came from Dr. Laura Schlessinger. I believe it, and I wanted my children to own that word! They also have to make reparations for the hurtful action.

Why the difference between home and school? At school, I am not the child's parent. But at home, I am and I want the child to be able to say, "I'm sorry." Each family has their own values and needs to share them with their children. If you don't share your family's values with your children, someone else will share theirs, and it may not be what you want them to learn. Your children need a solid foundation for life and surviving out in the "wild."

Miss Mona's advice — fighting fixes

1. Be sure the injured child is attended to first, and is allowed to make their needs known, and is able to tell the other child how they feel.
2. The hitting child needs to make amends in some way.
3. If it becomes a regular behavior, the hitting child may need thinking time or to lose a privilege.
4. What are your values? Teach them to your children.

BITING

Biting is most common among toddlers ages 1–3. It happens most often when your little one is angry or frustrated. Sometimes you can figure out why your toddler is biting. Toddlers experience big feelings just like the rest of us, but do not have the words they need to express themselves, which is why they often bite. Biting seems to be more common in boys than girls.

When my son Kyle was almost two years old, I went back to teaching part-time. I was working at a preschool that allowed me to bring my child to school with me. He even got to be in my class (mistake #1). I was working only in the afternoon and it was going to be great. Kyle would come with me and get to have a little preschool experience.

We had a short group time every afternoon, and one of the children, Jenny, sat on my lap each day. If you've ever taught in a classroom with your own child, and you recall that we're talking about biting here, I'm sure you can see where this is going.

Kyle bit the same little girl every day. It was very embarrassing. I tried all of my go-to remedies without success. He was still so little. Then I decided to try a reward system. If he didn't bite, he would get a small reward. This worked sometimes.

I remember driving home and we were having a conversation (as well as you can with an almost-two year old). We pulled into the driveway, I looked at him, and suddenly it hit me like a ton of bricks – Duh, Miss Mona! I said, "You don't like it when Jenny sits on my lap, do you?" He shook his head no. I apologized, and thought to myself, *How could I be so dense?* Of course he didn't like it. I'm *his mom*. From then on, no one sat on my lap, and Kyle never bit anyone again.

As your child gets more words, the biting should decrease. In the meantime, you can't have your child biting someone every time they are frustrated. What do you do? Stay calm, and remember less is more. I don't very often lead with a no when I am correcting children, but in this situation, stay calm and be firm. Most importantly, be consistent.

"Ouch, biting hurts!" or "No biting." A long explanation is not needed, nor will your toddler understand. Please go directly to the person who has been bitten. Take care of them first. Be sure to clean the area with soap and water. After you have attended to the bite, check on your toddler – who may be confused, not understanding that they actually hurt someone. However, if this has become a pattern or your child is using biting to get attention, you don't want to give too much attention to the biter. It's a fine line we parents and caregivers walk. Everyday.

Chapter 9

It's Not the Monster Under the Bed

"My alarm clock wears cute jammies and smiles at me when I wake up."

—Unknown

No, it definitely is not the monster under the bed. It's the crack monsters who come out of the closet when the door isn't closed all the way. Well, at least that's what my older sister told me when we shared a room way back when, and I'm pretty sure she believed it. This caused me to demand the closet door be completely closed, shut tight, no cracks whatsoever! This also gave my husband a really good laugh when we got married and he left the closet door open. He learned quickly to close the closet door.

Children are with their parents or another adult all day every day… then we have the nerve to put them to bed alone. No wonder putting our kids to bed can be such a nightmare. A bedtime routine can be a lifesaver, or at the very least a sleep saver.

Your bedtime routine should include gradual steps leading up to bedtime, and contain verbal and nonverbal clues that communicate bedtime is coming. Consistency, follow through, and routines make just about everything easier, including bedtime.

Your bedtime routine can begin when your child is brand new. Newborns do not, and I repeat do not, have regular sleep patterns. Their sleeping habits have nothing to do with day and night. (Miss Mona's advice – *Sleep when they sleep!*) At around 2–4 months they begin to settle in and *may* develop a more regular sleep pattern. However, you can still begin a bedtime routine.

Bedtime routines can start the day you bring baby home from the hospital. Since we know infants sleep when they need to, your new routine can be done at the time that one day will become bedtime. Please don't repeat the routine every two hours throughout the night and day.

Your routine can include whatever you like and need.

- Bath time
- Talking to baby
- Reading or telling a little story
- Feeding
- Putting the baby to bed

Your routine may change as your child gets older and possibly you have more children. Don't worry if you didn't start out with a routine; you can start now.

Some people like to have their baby sleep in bed with them, or in a bassinet or crib next to their bed, or in their own room down the hall. Not being perfect myself, I will not judge how you do it. Sleeping habits are very personal, and we all need our sleep!

A bedtime routine was really important to me, so my husband and I had one in mind before we brought Kyle home from the hospital. We did our best to establish a regular bedtime each night that started with a bath, then being cozy on the couch. "Cozy" was quiet time on the couch, and it changed through the years, but it happened after jammies were on and teeth brushed. Next was a quick drink and a trip to the bathroom. Then we went to his room where we read or made up a story. Finally there would be prayers, a hug, and a kiss goodnight.

Kyle, slept in a bassinet in our room near me. This way when he needed to be fed (I was nursing him) I could get to him easily and put him back down. I always tried to be sure he was still a little awake when I put him to bed, so if he woke up he would know where he was and wouldn't be afraid. In this way, he would be able to get himself back to sleep. I didn't want his crib to be a scary place.

I had read Dr. T. Berry Brazelton's book, *Sleep: The Brazelton Way,* and was a fan of his bedtime method. I didn't follow it totally, but the parts I used worked well for my family.

When Kyle did wake up during the night, I would nurse him but keep the talking to a minimum. This may sound sad but I wanted Kyle to learn the difference between day and night. In the day we talked and sang but at night it was quiet time. When he was finished nursing, he went right back to his bassinet.

The first time he slept through the night, he was about six weeks old, I woke up in the middle of the night and waited to hear him, then waited some more. I checked on him. He was beautifully, peacefully, sound asleep. I waited and checked a couple of times then got up and sat on the couch and read a book till about 5:00 A.M. when he finally woke. Believe it or not, I was a little sad when he slept through the night that first time, feeling he was getting big already and needing me less. I got over it. Sleep is good!

He did occasionally wake up during the night after this, and on those nights I would peek in at him or if needed, I would go in and just lay my hand on his back or pat him for a minute. But still no talking, because night is for sleeping. I look back now and wonder if this was harsh. However, it worked well for us. Kyle was always a great sleeper and had no problems with attachment. He may just have been the best sleeper ever.

Four years later, our second child, Madelynn, was also a bedside sleeper. I nursed her as well. She and Kyle weren't similar at all. Yes, I still believed in Dr. B's method, but the guilt monster got the best of me. I thought since Kyle had gotten so much one-on-one time, Maddie needed more attention, which seemed easiest to find in the middle of the night.

How could I possibly expect her to put herself to sleep? When she woke up... oh my, I would nurse her then set her on my lap and we would talk and smile. My husband was a sound sleeper! When I remember those nights now, I did enjoy it... but I was tired. Maddie was not a great sleeper then, and 23 years later she's still a night owl.

With child number three, Kaylee, the verbal one, she didn't like a pacifier or a bottle. Kaylee woke up in the night a lot. When sleep was in short supply, one will do whatever is needed to get it. For Kaylee we rocked, walked, jiggled, and patted. I also hummed to her while simultaneously swinging her in my arms. The tune was always the same, "Once Upon a Dream" from the Disney movie *Sleeping Beauty*. It was perfect for swinging her.

If you can imagine this scene it's the middle of the night, in the dark, after all the other methods have failed. The tired, now frustrated, me would cradle her in my arms bent over at the waist swinging her back and forth humming the soundtrack of *Sleeping Beauty*. This my husband could not sleep through, and learned fast not to laugh at me. He did often say, "You're going to send her flying out the window." But it helped get her to sleep.

We later discovered she liked white noise. A fan in her room was helpful on the nights when I learned to let her cry herself back to sleep (don't judge). It was probably more difficult for me than it was for her, but we knew she was safe, healthy, and not completely alone.

Today it is called sleep training, but 20 or so years ago it was just helping your baby learn to sleep. Each night the crying got shorter and shorter, but in the beginning, she would cry then stop, cry then stop, as if she was listening for us. Mike or I would go in lay our hand on her so she knew we were there but we did not pick her up or talk, then we would go out.

It was a difficult and tiring time, but we all got through it. I know some of you will say it's not good to let your baby cry, concerned that it causes babies stress and possible attachment or behavior issues. For Kaylee this method worked for us.

Recently I found a study from Flinders University in Adelaide, Australia, that compared three different sleep training methods: Graduated Extinction (crying it out), Bedtime Fading (putting baby to bed closer to the time they actually fall asleep), and the control group who had no sleep training but received information about infant sleep habits. The study found both sleep training methods seemed safe, in the short-term and long-term, and that levels of cortisol (stress hormone) were lower in the babies who had sleep training as opposed to the control group. One year later, the parents of the sleep trained babies reported no more problems with attachment or behavior than the control group.

As for Kaylee, she's a happy, well adjusted, just enough attached to me, and all around healthy human.

Michael, child number four – and sadly, our last – was so mellow. He had very little trouble sleeping. Or it could have been that I was so tired I didn't hear him, and he learned to sleep through the night on his own. He also slept in our room, and I remember nursing him in the middle of the night, but he was just such an easy baby. He has since grown up to also be a wonderful well-adjusted human.

How we sleep as a family, and how we help our babies learn to sleep is a personal, and emotional subject. There are so many theories on how to sleep, it's safe to say there is no perfect way that will work for every family or every baby, but there is a best way for you and your family. I had four babies and four very different experiences. My advice is simply to lead with love. Do your best, and be kind to yourself.

Miss Mona's advice
sleepy-time tips
— even if it's just you that's sleepy —

1. Have a bedtime routine.
2. Every child is different. Don't compare.
3. Do what works for your family.
4. Sleep is very important, for you and baby.
5. Sleep when baby sleeps.

FOOTNOTES:

Schum, Timothy R., et al. "Sequential acquisition of toilet-training skills: a descriptive study of gender and age differences in normal children." *Pediatrics 109*(3). March 2002.
https://pubmed.ncbi.nlm.nih.gov/11875176/

Storrs, Carina. "It's OK to let your baby cry himself to sleep, study finds." CNN, May 24, 2016.
https://www.cnn.com/2016/05/24/health/cry-it-out-sleep-training-ok/index.html

Chapter 10

There's a Stranger in My House:
My Teenager Doesn't Talk to Me Anymore

"Sometimes you will never know the value of a moment until it becomes a memory."
—Theodor Seuss Geisel, Dr. Seuss

I know you thought this book was about young children. Well, you're right, but conversations with your teenager don't magically happen when your child turns twelve. The conversations began when your teenager was born.

We need to talk *with* our children every day, even when they can't talk back. When I say *with*, I don't mean *to* them. There's a difference. I'm talking about a conversation of back and forth dialogue.

We want to be comfortable having any conversation with our children, but some are simply not comfortable and can even be awkward. When they're little, you're their whole world, and at this age they actually want to know what you think. Children often believe their parents are some kind of superhero. Yes, that's a difficult job to have and even harder to keep as they get older, because... say it with me, *"There's no perfect parent."* We eventually lose our shine.

You will do your very best to answer all of your child's questions, a seemingly never-ending list. It's best to answer these questions at your child's developmental level. When your three year old asks, "Where do babies come from?" they really do not want or need the whole truth! (Remember, "Talk less, smile more.") Keep it simple, they will ask again in a year or so, and again, and again. Each time you can (as you feel ready and they're mature enough), share a bit more of the story.

Please, when sharing any sensitive information with your own children – such as babies, Santa Claus, or the Tooth Fairy – explain to your children that this isn't something we need to share with our friends or other kids at school. Not because it's bad or wrong, but because this is something parents like to share with their own children.

When my girls were very young, a little friend shared with them where babies come from, a bit too early and with way too much detail. I'm not exaggerating when I say my daughters were horrified. This was not the way I had envisioned the conversation happening. They hadn't asked this friend; she just volunteered the information. The situation required us to have this conversation before the girls were ready for it... and definitely before I was ready. It went fine, but they were disturbed by the whole situation.

The important thing is to begin the conversation, whatever it is, and keep it going. This way, as your child gets older, talking with you won't be so weird or uncomfortable. My own mother was not good in this area, and it was uncomfortable, so I have tried to do this differently with my children.

When children become teenagers, some do want more privacy. They talk less, and hang out in their rooms a lot. It's important to find the balance, and keep the conversation going. Being a teenager today is much more difficult than when I was a teenager (back in the dark ages of no cell phone or internet). The drama and struggle is real. Sometimes you need to make them talk because you know something is just not right. At that point it's your duty.

How do you do this?

The answer is: *Dinner!*

Dinner

Having dinner, at the dining room table, with your family every night is where wonderful, and sometimes painful conversations happen. Ideally, dinner together should happen every night.

I know you're busy, or you work nights. It doesn't matter what you eat. Cereal can be a delicious and easy dinner. Start while they're little and it'll become a routine, then it will be a bit easier when life becomes truly busy!

If dinner together every night is impossible, try to find at least two or three nights a week when you can sit together at the end of the day, even if the meal is a delicious peanut butter sandwich.

I believe in dinner together so much it will probably be the subject of my next book. But if you really can't make it work for dinner, try breakfast. Get up fifteen minutes earlier, sit down, and start your day together.

Children and parents need this type of family connection. It keeps us all grounded and up to date on each other's lives. Because you are looking at each other and talking, if something is going on with your child, you are more likely to see it. Put the cell phones away and turn off the screens. (Pizza-and-a-movie night is the exception!) Give your time to each other. Eating together doesn't take that much time. Then get everyone involved in the clean-up – it can be fun. I remember doing the dishes with my dad. He always made me laugh, and loved to sing. We would talk and sing together. I didn't realize then, how much I loved that time.

Doing the dishes or cooking together can also be a great time for conversation. When your hands are busy, and you're not directly looking at each other, it's less confrontational. The more awkward or difficult discussions are easier and you can gain valuable insights into your child's life and dreams.

CAR RIDES

While you're busy trying to get errands done and driving your children to school, gymnastics, baseball, and on top of that dealing with traffic, it may not seem like the best conversation time. But let's take a step back and look at it from a different angle. Your child is trapped in the car with you. This can be a good thing, a blessing in disguise, a silver lining. Just like washing the dishes or cooking together, car rides – whether planned trips or errands – are a great time to talk.

Your hands are busy, and you definitely don't look at each other. Turn down the music and leave the TV screen off. This is an excellent time to learn more about your child, and they can learn about you too.

Not good at starting a conversation? Try starting with the basics: "I like…" or "I don't like…" or "I wish I had."

Or try talking about your favorites food, color, song, or sport.

Then go a bit deeper: "I like it when my friends…" or "I don't like it when my friends…"

The possibilities are literally endless. Take these opportunities to get to know the people you live with. The regular day-to-day things you do as a family and the traditions you share all help to build bonds and make the family connection even stronger.

TRADITIONS

The foods you eat on holidays and special occasions, the places you go, and the things you do as a family will become woven into the tapestry of your family history. Family traditions are important. They link us together, especially as children get older. Your kids will look forward to those things, and treasure how you celebrate birthdays and holidays.

My children have actually gotten upset when I have tried to change things up a bit. I don't even want to tell you about the wails and moans that erupted at the mere mention of an artificial Christmas tree. Needless to say, there is not a fake tree lurking in our attic.

Routines, are important here too. Think about the places you stop on the way to Grandma's house, the days of going to the park, playing board games, movie night, donuts after church, even just a nightly walk after dinner. All of these rituals become a part of us, a part of your family story. As your children get older, the routines sometimes morph or change, depending on the activities they are involved in, but do your best to hang on to some of them. They make for wonderful memories!

1. Remember to talk with and really look at your children every day.
2. Busy hands make awkward conversations more comfortable.
3. Traditions bind us together.

Chapter 11

It's All About You (Sometimes)

"Parents traveling with small children should first secure their own air masks and then their children's masks."

—Every airline you've flown on

Do you like this quote? Well, I thought it appropriate, funny, and true. It's also something I have been trying to learn to do for nearly three decades: take care of myself first! I'm definitely encouraging you to learn from my mistakes.

Why secure your own mask first? If you can't breathe, then you aren't much good to anyone.

It's true. I'm not saying you should spend all day at the gym or out with friends, but I am saying, like with everything else, you need to find the balance. Taking care of yourself gives you peace, and it also allows you to be able to share yourself. When your "cup" is full, you have more to give. When you feel depleted you get cranky (I know I do), and there is nothing left to share.

My mom once shared with me two really important things (well, lots of things really, but these two I remember vividly):

1. "Be careful who you date; you can't help who you fall in love with. You could end up married to them." If you're not married, that one totally applies to you, especially if you have children.
2. "Remember you two came first. The kids will eventually move out."

Her meaning? I needed to take care of myself and my marriage. I will need to know that person across the table from me in 30 years. This is where my husband and I are now, with just one child left at home who will be leaving soon. I think we did okay.

It's very important to find the time to take care of yourself and your relationships. Before our kids were born, I always said, "We came first, we will put ourselves first, weekly date nights, vacations just for us." Once Kyle was born, that promise didn't go *totally* out the window, just mostly. He didn't have a babysitter until he was about six months old.

When child number two, three, and four came along, it became more difficult to find time and energy for date night. Luckily, my husband is very good at remembering to take care of me and us! We also found a couple of really amazing babysitters, which made it so much easier to plan time away from the children.

Just so you know, one babysitter did just fine, even when she watched all four of them. She even did the dishes and picked up toys. By the way, she never fell asleep on the job. If you find an excellent babysitter, keep them and pay them well. It's worth it!

I can vividly remember a day when I desperately needed alone time. My exact words to Mike were, "If I could get to the dark side of the moon, I wouldn't be alone enough." During these times, he would immediately send me out of the house to do whatever. I usually went to a really good friend's house. Her three kids were older than mine, so she understood exactly what I was feeling.

This was so great and helpful. A better solution would have been for me to plan – actually schedule – time for myself each week. Self-care, or me-time may sound like a cliché, but it is absolutely necessary. When we are happy and relaxed, we are better parents, and all around better humans. Which makes it easier to be... wait for it... consistent and able to follow through. When we are tired and stressed, we are more likely to give in when our children whine or beg for things we wouldn't ordinarily allow just to get a minute of peace. We have all been there. We get cranky, grumpy, and feel deprived. Nobody likes a crabby parent.

It's important to be kind to yourself. Just in case you have forgotten how, here are a few ideas:

- Send your kid(s) to a friend's house. (Okay, here is where it gets good.)
- Do *not* go grocery shopping or clean the house!
- Stay home, be alone in your home.
- Paint your nails, take a long, uninterrupted shower or nap, bake something, watch something on TV (a show that's not for children).

None of this is expensive, and you, of course, will do the same for your friend next week. A side benefit I have found, and I am not alone in this, is when you have other children over to play, it's often a little easier than just your own one or two kids. It's true.

If your kids don't handle the weekly errands so well, then treat yourself to a sitter occasionally, or grandparents and aunts are wonderful and fun for little people to hang out with. The grandparents and aunts I see at my preschool love hanging out with their little people. While you're doing the errands it's okay to not set land speed records. Get a coffee and actually enjoy it!

Remember to schedule date nights or friend nights. If you are the primary caregiver for your family, *you* are the S.E.O. Senior Executive Officer in charge of Operations (that means everything). Companies understand that to be effective, you must have time off and away. Parenting is 24/7. Put yourself on your to-do list. It's not selfish, so don't feel guilty. I have reminded so many parents at school and myself of this. I have parents who occasionally drop their child off early to go to the gym. Their faces are full of guilt. Please don't feel guilty when taking care of yourself.

Helping Around the House

Confession: Vacuuming is my favorite household job. I love the look and feel of a freshly vacuumed living room. It's just so... beautiful! I totally understand you want a clean house. *But* it's okay to let the vacuuming, dusting, and dishes wait. They will all still be there. So, play Legos a little longer, help with the second puzzle, read just one more book, and have one more cup of pretend tea. Then let your kids help with the house clean-up. (I think I just heard a collective GASP.) Honestly, they can help, it gets done, and it can be fun. The 2–5-year-olds actually like to help, and they are capable of helping, just don't go crazy and give them the bleach. Do invest in a small broom, dustpan, and some microfiber cloths. It won't be *perfect*, but that's okay because we threw away that word.

Give the opportunity for children to feel proud of themselves and their work. Appreciate them and let them know they are helpful at making the house look nice. Let them pick up toys, shoes, papers, and sweep with a little broom and dust with their own cloth. Let your children help now, while they still think it's fun. Make it a game. You're helping them to build routines that could possibly last a lifetime. Then when you're finished, praise them for their work.

Life is messy. Parenting can be difficult. It's an around-the-clock job. I hope you have someone or a few someones to help you. It's a team effort: you, your spouse or partner, grandparents, aunts and uncles, caregivers and preschool teachers. Please reach out for help. It's not weak; it is vital for you and your children.

1. Schedule time for yourself.
2. Date Night or Friend Night is important.
3. Let your children help around the house.
4. No one and nothing is perfect.

Chapter 12

Fun

"In every job that must be done there is an element of fun." —Mary Poppins

We can get so caught up with work, school, and the daily household stuff, I sometimes think we forget to have fun with our kids. For now let's put away the behaviors and techniques to deal with behaviors, and instead let's talk about fun. Family fun is something we need to set aside time for every week and allow yourself to revel in the spontaneity. Your kids will remember your family fun times forever.

My kids often remind me of the things we did and the games we played when they were little. Several times a week we would all walk to the park around the corner. Their favorite game was essentially freeze tag, but we called it "The White Witch," from the books and movie *The Chronicles of Narnia*. (The film can be a bit scary so pre-read or watch before sharing with your children).

I was the Witch, which meant I was "It" and would chase them. Of course, chasing four children is tiring, but fun. In an effort to tag them I would tempt them with Turkish Delight (like in the movie). When they would stop running to get the "Turkish Delight" I would tag them. They waited frozen for one of their siblings to tag and unfreeze them. On very rare occasions I could catch them all. It was fun and great exercise for all of us!

"Lava," a game children play all over the world, was particularly enjoyed by my oldest, Kyle, who taught his younger sisters and brother. Basically the floor was "hot lava" and the idea was to see if you could get around the house without touching the floor.

I remember one time it had been a rainy week and we were stuck inside. I'm sure you know what that's like – everyone bouncing off the walls – so this was a fun and welcomed game. The rooms inside our house were laid out in a circle and the kids had to get around without touching the floor. They made a path of throw pillows, a footstool, a chair or two, and then swung on the closet door. They would jump from thing to thing. When they got to the hallway they stood on a chair (from the dinner table), put their feet on the closet door knobs while holding on to the top of the door, then swung the door to the next pillow or whatever the next safe thing was. It was super fun for them to do and for me to watch.

Adventure Sunday

Consider Adventure Sunday as a day to go to the park, maybe a movie, or a drive to somewhere out of your area for lunch. Whatever it is doesn't really matter. In my family it was just the fact that all six of us went together that made it a huge hit.

Adventure Sunday was special because it didn't happen every week. It was the weekend, so Dad got to be involved, which made it extra fun. It wasn't anything extravagant though, just that we were all together. Usually it included finding a new park or visiting an old favorite that was further from home. We loved parks, and still do actually. When there was a kid friendly movie, we would go to that or even just have lunch out. When you have kids, anything and everything is an adventure. The idea was always that we were together having fun.

CHECK-IN LUNCH

When you have more than one child it's essential to have some one-on-one time with each kid. This is something my husband and I did and still try to do with our children. We would arrange a "date" with the child whose turn it was, and the other three would go to the cousin's house or to Grandma and Grandpa's house which was fun too.

The day always included lunch, child's choice, and some kind of activity. Lunch was the most important part. As the kids got older my husband and I felt it was even more important to check in with each one. We could talk about anything, and no topic was off limits.

Conversations have become increasingly interesting as they have gotten older. One time, our oldest daughter took us out for a check-in lunch. We were a little nervous, but everything was fine.

CLEANING UP

With four homeschooled children, two adults, and two dogs, a house gets cluttered. Cleaning up is a necessary evil. You can make it fun, and a learning experience too. Make it a game to pick up the toys by color or by number. Try setting a timer and see how many toys can be put into a box before the timer rings. Music is fun too, so turn the music up and see if all the toys can be picked up before the song is over.

My husband is self-employed, and works from home. Occasionally his clients need to come to the house. I liked to know a day ahead of time, so I could be sure the toys were picked up and the house tidy, but sometimes I only got a 15–20 minute heads up. Making the clean-up fun, fast and painless was even more important on those days.

While our children were doing their schoolwork in the kitchen or playing in various parts of the house, my husband would occasionally say, "Oh, by the way, a client is coming by in about 15 minutes." I would literally stand in the middle of the house and call, "All hands on deck." Everyone knew what it meant. The kids would come running from wherever and whatever, and we would pick up everything as fast as we could. It didn't matter whose stuff it was – it just needed to go away. It was actually fun, and the clean-up was done amazingly fast.

Whatever it is that your family enjoys can become the basis for wonderful traditions and memories. The goal of this little chapter is to remind you to play and laugh each day, and to find the joy in everyday things. Fun doesn't have to be expensive or elaborate. It can be as simple as playing a game, taking a walk, or sharing an ice cream. I know you've heard the saying "They grow up so fast," but it's true. Enjoy your children and family time. You'll never regret it!

Miss Mona's advice — family fun ideas

1. Schedule it, so your family fun doesn't get lost in the busy.
2. Keep it simple. It doesn't have to be expensive or cost at all.
3. Play in the rain, snow, and mud.
4. Have a spontaneous Dance Party.
5. Cook or bake.
6. When you take photos, print them (or send them off to one of those amazing companies that puts your photos in little books).

Chapter 13

Last Thoughts

"The world is changed by your example, not by your opinion." —Paulo Coelho

Throughout this little book I have shared bits of me and my children – the ones I birthed and the preschool ones. I hope you have enjoyed it and picked up a few helpful tidbits.

Looking back, which is sometimes heart wrenching, as all my little ones are now big, I'm happy with our family and how my husband and I have raised and taught our children. We aren't perfect… there have been mistakes along the way, and I'm sure there are more to come, as we're now learning how to parent or not parent our adult children.

Mike and I have always tried our best, mistakes and all, to parent from a place of intense, wholehearted, want nothing but the best for you, love. If you didn't get to grow up in your "ideal" family (really no one does), and especially if your childhood was difficult, you do get another chance, with your children, your own family.

No matter where or how you grew up, remember no one and nothing is perfect. If you need help, don't be afraid to reach out and ask.

When my children were little I was always asking friends: How do you? Why do you? When do you? In fact I'm still asking. Pediatricians, caregivers, and grandparents, all have a wealth of information. All you need to do is ask. Don't be embarrassed. Raising children and growing a family takes time, a precious commodity. If you spend it well, it will be worth its weight in gold.

As I said in the beginning, this book is meant to be a conversation like I would have with a friend or one of my preschool parents. Hopefully I have accomplished that goal. I would love to continue the conversation.

You can find me on Facebook @Miss Mona's Advice for Mothers, Fathers & Caregivers, or join my email list at that same address.

If you've gotten this far, Thank You!
I know what you are thinking... *Now what do I do?*

Connect with me
so we can continue the conversation.

@MissMonasAdvice

---

*"Imperfections are not inadequacies.
They are reminders that we're all in
this together."* —Brene Brown

Miss Mona's
Method MasterClass

Does your child listen to you?

Are you feeling frantic and overwhelmed?

Master Miss Mona's methods and techniques
in this fast and fun MasterClass.

Her 30-year experience with parents and children
has formed methods that work wonders...
so you can have a peaceful, happy home!

---

www.MissMonasMethod.com

$100 discount for book owners

Acknowledgments

It takes a team of people to get a book from start to finish. Thank you so much to those first few I was brave enough to tell that I was writing a book: Mike, Nicole, Liz, Debbie, Julia. Without your regular "How's your book going?" it wouldn't be here.

My amazing editors: Kaylee, Demi, Donna. Thank you for the word/grammar makeover! You make me sound better than I would otherwise. To Demi, again, and your own team of magicians who have brought the pages to life and made them beautiful to look at.

To Mimi S., you are an amazing cheerleader paving the way for my book and helping me share Miss Mona with the world.

To those whom I never saw or spoke to, but who put the physical book together, Thank you.

To the trees who made the paper.

Ultimately, to God, for making all things possible.

www.ingramcontent.com/pod-product-compliance
Lightning Source LLC
LaVergne TN
LVHW052255070426
835507LV00035B/2907